Jesus in the World Today

Jesus in the World Today

Poetry and Prose About Jesus for the Twenty-First Century

SARA JEWELL

RESOURCE *Publications* · Eugene, Oregon

JESUS IN THE WORLD TODAY
Poetry and Prose About Jesus for the Twenty-First Century

Copyright © 2025 Sara Jewell. All rights reserved. Except for brief quotations in critical publications or reviews, no part of this book may be reproduced in any manner without prior written permission from the publisher. Write: Permissions, Wipf and Stock Publishers, 199 W. 8th Ave., Suite 3, Eugene, OR 97401.

Resource Publications
An Imprint of Wipf and Stock Publishers
199 W. 8th Ave., Suite 3
Eugene, OR 97401

www.wipfandstock.com

PAPERBACK ISBN: 979-8-3852-4845-2
HARDCOVER ISBN: 979-8-3852-4846-9
EBOOK ISBN: 979-8-3852-4847-6

Scripture quotations marked TLB are from *The Living Bible* copyright © 1971 by Tyndale House Foundation. Used by permission of Tyndale House Publishers Inc., Carol Stream, Illinois 60188. All rights reserved.

Scripture quotations marked NIV are from the *New International Version*® NIV® Copyright © 1973, 1978, 1984, 2011 by Biblica, Inc. Used with permission. All rights reserved worldwide.

Scripture quotations marked ESV are from the ESV®Bible (The Holy Bible, English Standard Version®), copyright© 2001 by Crossway Bibles, a publishing ministry of Good News Publishers. Used by permission. All rights reserved.

Scripture quotations marked NRSVU are taken from the *New Revised Standard Version Updated* Edition. Copyright © 2021 National Council of Churches of Christ in the United States of America. Used by permission. All rights reserved worldwide.

Scripture quotations marked CEB are from the COMMON ENGLISH BIBLE. © Copyright 2011. COMMON ENGLISH BIBLE. All rights reserved. Used by permission.

A version of "The World Needs More Jesus" appeared in the anthology, *Following Jesus Today: Stories and Reflections*, edited by Rob Fennell, 2023.

Cover art © Norene Smiley / norenesmiley.com

Contents

Acknowledgements vii

Introduction 1
    At the East Side Diner 4

1. The World Needs More Jesus 7
    Jesus Is Weird 12

2. Knock, Knock (You Know Who's There) 16
    Waiting in the Streets 21

3. Doing "Jesusy" Things 24
    Come As You Are 28

4. We Hope It's Not Jesus 31
    Red Tape 36

5. When Hope Becomes Subversive 39
    The Empire 44
    Those People 47

6. What If? 50
    Politically Motivated 55

7. Jesus Is Political 58
    Where Are You? 62
    The Shores of Sabratha 66

8. Blessed Are the Fixers 69
    Reckoning 75
    Raging in the Streets 77

Contents

9. Turn the Other Cheek 79
    The Protest 84
10. Love the Earth 87
    Jesus, Take the Wheel 92
    Heaven on Earth 95
11. Plant What Will Grow 99
    Planting Seeds 103
    Calling in the Streets 106
12. Where Is Your Treasure? 108
    Jesus' Birthday 112
    Dancing in the Streets 116
13. It Doesn't Add Up 118
    The Encampment 125
    After Christmas 128
14. Build a Bigger Table 131
    Birthday Parties in the Park 135
    Who Do You Say I Am? 137
15. Audacious Women 140
    Reminders 145
16. Who Are You Looking For? 147
    Were You There 150
    In the Garden 153
17. Just Say Yes 156
    Consider the Ice Cream Cone 160
18. Part of Jesus' Family 162
    Son of Man's Best Friend 167
19. Healing Touch, Healing Tears 170
    Healing in the Streets 175
20. Grace Is Snacks and a Nap 177
    Blessings for the 21st Century 182

Afterword: I Can See Clearly Now 187

Notes 191

Bibliography 197

Acknowledgements

I LIVE, WORK, AND write on the traditional and unceded territory of the Mi'kmaq. I am grateful that the eternal spirit and energy of the Indigenous peoples flow through this land, and show me the way of peace, understanding, and reconciliation. *Wela'lioq*

It takes a bunch of lovely, patient, and generous people to help a writer create and publish. With all my heart, soul, mind, and strength, I offer love and gratitude to:

-Editor Michael Schwartzentruber. Our second book together. Thank you for your wisdom and guidance.

-Terry Paul Choyce. Thank you for believing this book belongs in the world.

-Rev. Catherine MacDonald, Rev. Katherine Burgess, and the CASA: An Experiment In Doing Church Online Facebook group.

-Artist Norene Smiley of Pugwash, Nova Scotia. I'm delighted to have one of your latest paintings, *Pilgrims: Migration to the Rim*, for the cover of this book.

-My writing mentor and friend, Marjorie Simmins. Thank you for your encouragement and excellent lunches.

-My best friend Sarah Whaley. Thank you for being the anchor when my boat is rocked by storms. A walk with our dogs is long overdue.

-My mother, Lynda. Thank you for listening to every single Jesus poem as I created them.

-My husband, Dwayne. Thank you for making sure there's always cream for my coffee.

Acknowledgements

-Wipf and Stock Publishers. You made a path into the world for this weird mix of poetry and prose. Thank you.

- My readers. You are the heart and soul of this book, and through your strength, may there be more Jesus in the world. xo

Introduction

IN JANUARY 2021, A minister familiar with my writing, who was also part of an online church community on Facebook, contacted me to see if I would take over her day to contribute. A decade earlier, when the Facebook group was created, the main requirement for each person was to write and post a morning and evening prayer on an assigned day.

At the time, writing prayers wasn't something that came easily to me, but I figured I could handle writing a morning and an evening prayer once a month, and it would help me develop that skill.

My first posting day was a Saturday, the day before Palm Sunday. As my debut in the group approached, I didn't have a clue what I would write. I was used to writing to a theme or to the idea of a worship service and had no idea what to write for a random Saturday. At that point, I was thinking that one prayer posted in the morning might have to cover the whole day.

On the Thursday before, the dog and I went for our afternoon walk and as we turned around at the creek to go home, all of a sudden, a poem dropped into my head. Not just the *idea* for a poem, but the whole poem—a poem about Jesus sitting in a diner with his twelve friends listening to them plan their arrival in Jerusalem the next day. A poem set in modern times. In a diner. With white coffee mugs. And a tour bus.

After hurrying home, I headed upstairs to my writing room and sat down at my desk. The whole poem poured out of me at once. Even the title came easily. I realized I had to write a poem for the group. Whatever I might write, it could come out of me no other way. I couldn't pass it off as a prayer; it was very clearly a poem.

This was the first of what I call my "Jesus poems," poems written about the life of Jesus in the twenty-first century—living in our world, doing the things we do, but of course doing them as Jesus would do. Jesus in a garden. Jesus at church. Jesus walking his dog along the street at night. Jesus feeling the pain of the world, of the people, in the scars in his palms. Jesus reminding us why we are here. There are a few exceptions where the poems are addressed to Jesus.

What they all have in common is that the language and the ideas are contemporary. Jesus for the twenty-first century.

Plenty of books have been written about the Bible, about the scriptures; about the Gospels, and the cultural context of Jesus' stories and of Paul's letters; about time and place, languages and translations. Jesus comes to me here and now. In my time and my place, in my language, in the stories I hear and read—like the story about the businessman riding on a subway in winter who noticed the holes in the shoes of the man across the aisle from him, and who handed over his winter boots and a pair of clean socks.

For me, it's essential to bring Jesus forward into our modern times. I don't know a lot of shepherds, do you? And how many of us hang out at wells collecting water? Placing Jesus in the midst of a protest makes a lot more sense to me. This is just another way of experiencing Jesus, of bringing him into our hearts and minds. We need to witness him alive and well in our context, in our world.

In my fourth year of providing worship services as a lay leader, the idea that "the world needs more Jesus" came to me, followed by 1) the sudden understanding that I finally had found the way I relate to the life and work of Jesus, and 2) this would be the guiding phrase of my spiritual writing. More and more, my messages focused on how we could better follow Jesus in our modern world. For me, Jesus remains utterly relevant; I find him invigorating and inspiring.In my eighth year of leading worship, when I was doing what I called an "Alphabet of Faith" sermon series (26 Sundays),

INTRODUCTION

I challenged myself to write my own prayers rather than use or adapt someone else's. Mingling those two factors—focusing on a contemporary Jesus and writing prayers—produced in my subconscious writing mind a special creative energy that birthed the Jesus poems. Like so much of my spiritual writing, these poems just come to me. I sit in front of a blank screen, poise my fingers over the keyboard, and with the hint of an idea, try to keep my conscious thinking to a minimum as I start to type. It's an amazing feeling and an amazing experience for a writer. I don't understand it; it really will be the unsolved mystery of my life, but I trust the process implicitly and am grateful for it.

My best friend keeps telling me it's simply the Holy Spirit at work in and through me.

No matter what, it's all an exquisite mystery. It's all energy and spirit, and going out not knowing but trusting the creative process and the source for inspiration. That's the greatest thing about it; there's room in that mystery for everyone to find Jesus in their own way, in their own context, in their own need to understand why he's still so relevant and necessary today.

I feel as if Diana Butler Bass, writing in her memoir about rediscovering Jesus, gives her blessing: "Your experience of Jesus matters. It matters in conversation with the 'big names,' when you argue with the tradition, and when you read the words and texts for yourself... The Jesuses you have known and the Jesus you know matter."[1] This collection of poems and reflections inspired by the way I experience Jesus is a work of heart in a world that needs more Jesus, especially a twenty-first century Jesus. He matters more than ever.

AT THE EASTSIDE DINER

On this day
Jesus and his friends
all of them
even those who worked an overnight shift
gather early at a diner
filling up the space
dragging over another table, adding a few more chairs
as each one arrives
hanging up coats
ordering coffee and toast

They are excited, even those who are yawning
and complaining about a breakfast meeting
they eat and drink
and a few hangovers dissipate

Jesus sits in the middle
with his fingers wrapped around a thick white mug
half-full
listening to his friends talk about tomorrow

They are planning, he thinks
planning, like it's a show—
a parade

"A convertible," someone suggests, "just like the politicians use!"
"Yeah, optimum visibility. Good idea," another agrees

Jesus sips his coffee

At the Eastside Diner

"We need flags for people to wave."
"Do we have a flag?"
"I can design one on this napkin. Who's got a pen?"
"Put a sword on the flag!"

Jesus sips his coffee

"I'm going to buy a new outfit for tomorrow."
"Not new. Go to the thrift shop. We need to save money for the food bank."
"My forsythia branches are blooming. I'll walk alongside and wave those."

The waitress comes over to Jesus
"What do you need, dear?" she asks. "Let me freshen up your coffee."
she fills his cup
"I'll bring you some more toast," she says. "My treat."

He thanks her,
and sips his coffee
it scalds his tongue

"I will ride the bus," Jesus says
his quiet voice cutting into the loud discussion
his friends stare at him

"I will ride the bus."

They all start talking at once
objecting, insisting, wondering
what on earth he's thinking
riding the bus into the city

"You need to make the right impression."
"A show of power, that's what we need right now."
"Oh, wait, you mean like a tour bus! Cool."

Jesus in the World Today

"No," Jesus says. "I will ride the number 3 bus into the city."

The bus, he thinks,
that's where my people are
not the politicians or the bureaucrats, not the investment bankers
you'd never catch that pastor in the Gucci suit
using public transit
the bus, he thinks
that's where I'll find the people who will follow me

"There's more than enough room for everyone
on the number 3 bus," he says

The waitress puts a plate of toast in front of Jesus
then holds out her hand
three packages of jam rest there
Jesus takes them
brushing his fingers over the heart line
that runs across the top of her palm
as he thanks her for her gift

1. The World Needs More Jesus[2]

IN MY WORK AS a lay worship leader, I first used the expression "the world needs more Jesus" in a church message in October 2016. The day's scripture reading was the story of Jesus healing a man possessed by demons. This is what Jesus said to the man after he healed him: "Go home to your friends and tell them what wonderful things God has done for you."[3]

In other words, go and tell your story.

My message that Sunday was about storytelling, about how storytelling is a basic human instinct. We need to tell our own stories, and we need to listen to other stories because that's how we come to understand ourselves and each other. That's how we make sense of the world.

Storytelling creates understanding and acceptance; it creates compassion and unity.

Storytelling is the way Jesus created and called disciples and it's the way we become his followers.

In that 2016 message, I wrote, "Jesus was a revolutionary, and if we follow him, we need to follow his way. We need to be radical and obvious and outspoken in order to remind the world, and the church, why we follow Jesus and why the *world* needs more Jesus."

That line—the world needs more Jesus—hit the tuning fork in my heart and it hasn't stopped vibrating since. It's why I want more stories about Jesus, why I want more of his stories. They're how I found a way to follow Jesus that resonated with me. The way I talk about Jesus may not be the way other people talk about

Jesus or relate to him, but it's how his words affect my heart and my spirit.

I was born and raised in The United Church of Canada. The congregation of my childhood in the 1970s was vibrant and active, full of children and young people. My memories aren't of Sunday school but of the weekend retreats at our local church camp, of the Christmas Eve pageants, and of the youth group's production of Marlo Thomas' children's revue, *Free to Be You and Me*. Music and creativity, laughter and conversation, hanging out with other families—just like we were one big family.

It was our minister at the time, however, who gave me my first impression of Jesus when I was four or five years-old (meaning, in my formative years). Garth couldn't have looked less like the long-haired, white-skinned Jesus with the patrician nose pictured in our books and hanging on our church walls. Garth had short, curly brown hair and he wore glasses. But, on Sunday mornings, he wore a long white gown and waved his arms around when he spoke, and I think that's where the connection began for me, the young concrete thinker. He was a dynamic speaker, passionate and animated. He also was a close family friend and flooded our quiet lives with his energy and intelligence. He was particularly fond of our "Little Red Renault," the cheap, basic compact car my father bought in 1976 for my mother. With its stick shift and bright color, it was a fun little car and Garth loved to drive it, borrowing it whenever his wife had their station wagon.

Some of this comes to me as a story; I don't actually remember these young years as clearly as I wish I did. But as a writer I understand how deeply our memories reside, even if our conscious mind can't access them.

Despite this vibrant and compelling early influence, by the time I reached my teens we lived in a different town and attended a different church. The male ministers were dull, unrelatable and uninspiring, easy to tune out. They didn't animate their gowns or their sermons. That's when I lost Jesus, and his passion and energy for his message and mission. He was no longer at church. He was no longer in my life. It would be thirty years before I rediscovered him.

It might not have happened if certain events had not unfolded as they did: if I had not moved to rural Nova Scotia, if I had not grown tired of being a substitute high school teacher, if I had not taken a job at the local community newspaper where one of my duties was updating the weekly church notices feature. That's how I noticed one church had a different minister listed every week. I emailed my contact and told her I could provide a worship service or two whenever they needed someone. In an area where ministers can be hard to find, my one or two services turned into a steady gig for more than ten years. I'm now licensed as a lay worship leader.

To this work I brought my skills as a journalist (researching and writing) and the mind of a faith seeker (doubting and wondering). Both of whom ask, "Why?" a lot.

One big question kept nagging at me: *Why do we reference the Hebrew scriptures so much?* In my new journey creating worship services, it frustrated me to have stories illustrating Jesus' new way and new truth (which, let's be honest, are not new 2,000 years later), yet the stories and prophets in the Hebrew scriptures seemed to be given as much, if not more, weight than Jesus' one overarching commandment. Why?

While attending church was a weekly practice for my family when I was growing up, we didn't sit at the dining room table and read the Bible then discuss it. The only time I recall anyone quoting the Bible was my mother saying, "Get thee behind me, Satan," as she held out her glass for another pour of wine. Perhaps if I'd read the Hebrew scriptures, if I knew all those ancient stories about the people of Israel, if I'd been told they were important and essential, or better, poetic and metaphorical, universal and ageless, I might feel some attachment to them, some loyalty and devotion, a connection. But that's not the case.

This is part of the reason I'm not interested in studying to be a minister. I couldn't finish an introductory course called Christian Theology because I got so annoyed at how the early church was constructed and the scriptures manipulated that I knew there was no way I could do a traditional theological degree. I wanted *more* Jesus, not less.

I understand that the Hebrew scriptures are part of Jesus' religious education, but my educational path began when I discovered contemporary progressive Christian writers (my favorite authors are women), who wrote about the kinds of ideas Garth was interested in back in the 1970s. At some point, I discovered that what is written about Jesus is the testament (a statement of belief) by other people to the life and ministry of Jesus, but that his message is a covenant—a new agreement between God and humanity. Jesus represents a new way of relating to God and to each other. Love one another the way I have loved you, Jesus said, and be unified by this love. That idea, combined with my belief that the world needs more Jesus, is how I found Jesus again.

As soon as I started to think about Jesus as a new covenant, as soon as I realized that "I come to fulfill the law" means those ten commandments can be set aside because the new law is based on Jesus' commandments, it all made sense.

I understood I wasn't the one who had lost the plot of the Jesus story; it was never properly explained to me in the first place. The Hebrew scriptures are important; they tell a history of the culture and people from which and in which Jesus grew and learned, but they aren't more important than Jesus and his ministry.

I grew up seeing Jesus (in the form of my minister, Garth) alive and well, waving his arms in the sanctuary and driving our little red car and picnicking in the park by the lake. I was raised with the embodiment of Jesus, the man, the minister, the teacher, the preacher.

I grew up with a contemporary Jesus—here and now, busy in the world doing and saying "Jesusy" things, being the Jesus the world needs more of. In the first century and in the twenty-first century.

But the best part is that when I found Jesus again, I discovered him in myself rather than in someone else. I found him in my own ideas and my own beliefs, in my own words and in my own work, in my own hopes for my life and in the world. Now I understand the stories. Now I can relate to the stories. I see the stories all around me and know why I believe the world needs more Jesus.

Now I can go and tell my story.

JESUS IS WEIRD

Apparently
September 9 is Wonderful Weirdos Day

I would not joke about something like that

especially since I woke up at 4:30 in the morning
on that day
with a message called "Jesus Is Weird"
demanding to be written down immediately

The creative Spirit may not understand
about sleeping in on Saturday morning
but the holy Spirit knows when a message
is needed more than ever

So here's that morning message
(and if anyone wants me to preach on or before September 9
I am available for all your radical Jesus messaging):

A lot of my spiritual writing places Jesus in the world today
takes him out of the Bible
where he's ignored in favor of
other stories, other people, other laws
rather than his law of love

because that law is weird

Love your neighbor?
Love your *enemy*?

Jesus Is Weird

Turn the other cheek
give your coat *and* your shirt
sell all your possessions, in fact,
welcome strangers and then
feed and clothe and house them
everyone, in fact?

What world is he living in?

I listened to an interview on the radio
with a university student
who was forced into couch-surfing during April exams
already a very stressful time of year
and she didn't find accommodations until the first of September
five months later
her experience with homelessness
gave her a fierce commitment to
providing a couch and a meal
to any student who needs them

That's weird, right?
welcoming strangers into your home
to feed them and give them a place to sleep?

Funny how weird
is exactly what Jesus wants us to do

Funny how weird
seems to be a synonym for
kind
merciful
fair
peaceful
welcoming
inclusive
worthy

Jesus in the World Today

Jesus was a guy
who wanted to change the world
not through a violent uprising
not with an army and a war
not with cruise missiles and cluster bombs
drones and collateral damage
not with secret police and black sites
the army and martial law
not with bullying and threats
misinformation and lies
he certainly didn't want to change the world
through white supremacy
but
through true liberation
based on the law of
love

Love? Really? That seems a little...
unrealistic

Yet consider what love actually is:
mercy and justice and humility
forgiveness and reconciliation
right relations
hospitality
gratitude
dignity

offering help hope and healing
with grace courage and wisdom

What the world needs now is
more love
more Jesus
more weirdness

Jesus Is Weird

After all
in a world where you can be anything

be weird

2. Knock, Knock
(You Know Who's There)

ONE SUNDAY MORNING WHEN I was leading worship at a church, the scripture readings were a collection of verses about how we are to take care of each other, including the following verses from the letter to the Hebrews: "Let us consider how to provoke one another to love and good deeds, not neglecting to meet together, as is the habit of some, but encouraging one another."[4]

Although I had read them at home and had selected them for the collection, they landed in a completely different way as I listened to someone else say these two verses out loud. My brain condensed the two verses into "Provoke love," a phrase that stuck in my head for so long I had to get it printed on a T-shirt.

Provoke love. What a Jesusy thing to do, to provoke love in one another. To provoke. To love. To do what Jesus asked of us and love our neighbors and take care of each other. By provoking one another.

I love the word "provoke"; I mean, it's so provocative, right? Webster's definition says, "To call forth a feeling or an action. To stir up purposely."[5]

There's another two-word combination that doesn't get enough airtime and it, too, deserves to be on a T-shirt. Jesus speaks it but there is only one translation of the Bible, the New International Version (*NIV*), that uses these exact two words: "shameless audacity." Other translations use words like persistence (*NRSVUE*), boldness (*CSB*), brashness (*CEB*), and even impudence

Knock, Knock (You Know Who's There)

(*ESV*), but none of those vibrate with passion and energy like the phrase "shameless audacity."

These phrases are found in the story Jesus tells about a man awakened at midnight by a neighbor banging on his door, needing food for hungry travelers. The man refuses, saying everyone in his house is in bed, asleep, and he won't help.

Jesus says, "Even though [the man] will not get up and give you the bread because of friendship, because of your shameless audacity, he will surely get up and give you as much as you need."[6]

Since Jesus tells this story right after he teaches the disciples how to pray, the parable is often understood as a call to persistent prayer: Don't give up, keep praying, your prayers will be answered. It is understood we are praying to God and expecting God to hear and answer our prayers.

Author and activist Craig Greenfield doesn't think this is the point of the story. He says that the cold-hearted neighbor who refused to help isn't God at all, but rather the powerful, wealthy, and elite of this world, and that the neighbor's answer to the knock on his door sounds like the response of an unjust government, or an insurance company, or a politician.[7]

We don't need shameless audacity to pray for the strength and courage to love our neighbors and to take care of each other; according to Greenfield, we need it—along with persistence and boldness and brashness—to take the needs of the world to those who have the power and resources to respond, to speak out against injustice and inequality, to get out of bed and fight for what's right.

Greenfield says, "Isn't it interesting then that the *very next* command Jesus gives is, 'Ask—and it shall be given, seek and you will find, knock and the door will be opened (Luke 11:9). In the context of this story, those words take on a radical new meaning, right?"[8]

Now, there's a familiar word when it comes to the work of Jesus.

Radical: Favoring extreme changes in existing views, habits, conditions, or institutions. Associated with political views, practices, and policies of extreme change.[9]

It also means having strong convictions, but over time the word radical became a negative trait; calling someone a radical is now a way of dismissing them as a person who won't stop knocking, who seeks to change the way we've always done things, who wants to flip tables and turn the established norms upside-down.

We know that idea: the upside-down gospel of Jesus most easily witnessed in his blessing the poor in spirit, those searching for ethics and morality, and the persecuted—those who ask, seek, and knock for peace, mercy and justice. He rejected the kind of popularity, power, and prosperity that was used to denigrate and deny others. At the very heart of the upside-down gospel of Jesus is the call to "do everything in love,"[10] where love is kindness, compassion, acceptance. Fairness. Hospitality. Inclusion. Comfort. Healing. Hope. An open door. A bigger table. A welcome from, and for, a stranger.

To those who have the power and resources to help others but refuse to do so, who turn their cheek so they don't have to see or hear, the command to love others is considered radical. The kind of radical that can be ignored.

In a world that needs Jesus more than ever, I'm so glad he remains as radical today as he was when he was a wandering preacher whose self-proclaimed purpose, based on his strong convictions about love, was to turn the world upside-down and create a new way of living based on a new truth. Jesus wanted to shake things up in ways that would actually change people's lives, but not with violence, or war, or oppression. Even though he gave commands, he wasn't a commander-in-chief with an army at his disposal; he was a donkey-riding carpenter who was a teacher, not a fighter. His commands were to love God and to love one another.

And we all know that loving someone—offering kindness and support no matter who, no matter what—is a lot harder than judging them and rejecting them. Jesus knew this, too, which is why he warned people that following him (then and now) would likely cost them friends and family.[11] In today's world, Jesus tells us there's no point in following him if we're not prepared to speak up at family dinners and backyard BBQs; in boardrooms and classrooms; when our friends and family, colleagues and classmates, start condemning people and policies that support and lift up "those people"—whoever it is they don't see as deserving compassion, mercy, and justice, food, shelter, and safety.

Love, and faith, mean not being afraid; or being afraid (and being radical) and saying it anyway, whatever the cost, however much it rocks the boat.

We all know about Jesus and boats, right? Jesus, waking up from his nap in a boat *during a storm*, and saying, "You of little faith. Why are you so afraid?"[12] I always think Jesus sounds just the teeniest bit cranky at being awakened from a nap by people who are freaking out for no reason. We all know storms, no matter how devastating, don't last.

He just wants us to have faith, and I don't think he's even looking for 100% faith; he'd be happy for us to have enough faith. In him. In love. In ourselves following him and harnessing the power of love. That's all we need: enough faith to make us ask, seek, knock. Enough faith to ask and seek and knock with shameless audacity. Never giving up. We don't change the world one inquiry, one meeting, one door opening at a time without a little faith and a lot of audacity. What's more challenging, do you think? Faith or audacity?

Audacity: Intrepid boldness. A bold or arrogant disregard for normal restraints.[13]

A word that makes people prickly the same way *radical* does. It might invoke the response, "How dare you?"

Daring. Bold. Persistent. Audacious. Radical. Shameless.

Surely that's not too much to ask of us? Of course, if you're an introvert like me, and like half of the population of the United States,[14] that's asking to receive a lot.

In her essay about living by a love ethic, Bell Hooks writes, "Faith enables us to move past fear. We can collectively regain our faith in the transformative power of love by cultivating courage, the strength to stand up for what we believe in, to be accountable in both word and deed."[15]

After all, this is no time to be like a turtle and hunker down in our shells, hoping someone else will do the asking, seeking, and knocking; hoping someone else has the shameless audacity to provoke love in others.

Well, you know who it is whose knocking on your shell, right?

That's Jesus saying in his very Jesusy way, "Don't be afraid. Come and follow me. You already have what you need in the midst of you, inside of you. Don't give up. Be audacious!"

All the introverts just pulled their heads back in their shells.
Knock, knock.
Who's there?
Doris.
Doris who?
Doris locked. That's why I'm knocking.

I think Jesus might have also said, "Don't lose your sense of humor. Laugh as often as you cry. Love your neighbors and your enemies, and don't give up."

He was shameless that way.

When I first started writing this piece and looked up the definition of "radical," I discovered that the first definition of the word has nothing to do with extreme change but with botany[16] (and also can be spelled "radicle"). It's the first root to appear when a seed germinates. This primary root grows downward into the soil, anchoring the seedling.[17] What better definition of Jesus could we find than he is the first radical of our faith? He is the primary root of the seed of love he planted. He anchors us in our faith—a faith based on the teachings of a person who called for great social and political change, the anchor that holds the seed as it grows into a plant that blooms where it's planted, that persists, that provokes love.

WAITING IN THE STREETS

(Inspired by verse 1 of the hymn, "Jesus Christ Is Waiting," by John L. Bell)

Jesus,
you are waiting for us.

Waiting for us to open our eyes
and notice the suffering of others
who seek only to be safe and secure
to be warm enough, fed enough, clothed enough, loved enough
to be welcomed, accepted, included
to be taken care of, cared for, cared about.

Waiting for us to open our ears
to hear the cries of
the abused and the abandoned
the weak and the wounded
to hear the pleas of
the broken and the burdened
the worried and the wronged
to stop talking and hear the truth
without defending
to listen and acknowledge the truth
without discounting.

Waiting for us to open our hearts
and speak words of support and encouragement
rather than judgment and humiliation,
to offer the compassion and peace and justice
the dignity
all humans deserve,

Jesus in the World Today

no matter who they are or what they have done
no matter how much is in their bank account.

Waiting for us to open our arms
and welcome
the stranger and the struggling
the mourning and the manic
the forgotten and the forgiven
to accept each person as they are in the moment they appear before us
just as Jesus accepted
the child, the woman and the tax collector
the dying, the doubting and the different.

Jesus, you with the heart filled with mercy and grace,
you are waiting for us
still
in stillness
with bated breath
and eternal hope
to be who you know we can be
to be better neighbors
better friends
better followers of you
who shows us the Way of Love
here and now
where we stand on this holy ground.

You are waiting for us
to let go of the ways we think it should be done
and do it your way instead
to see ourselves reflected in the eyes of
each person around us on the streets
not just the ones sitting next to us in the pews
to live the commandment to love one another
without hesitation
without conditions

without expecting anything in return.

We pray
in the name of all those we have
ignored and rejected and punished
but who are beloved by you.

Amen

3. Doing "Jesusy" Things

EARLY IN MY WORK as a lay worship leader, I started collecting stories featuring Jesus in the world today, as in, stories featuring ordinary people acting like Jesus. If I was going to say the world needs more Jesus, and if I was going to talk about Jesus in the world today, I needed to be able to provide evidence, give examples.

If we keep our eyes and ears open, we will discover a lot of people doing Jesusy things (thank goodness): people riding subways or commuter trains, people standing in line at the convenience store, eating in restaurants, shopping at the mall. Sometimes a story is so aged to perfection I'm skeptical about its veracity, but, at the same time, those stories can be so breathtakingly beautiful I choose to believe them because we need them. And you know, we only need two or three examples to start seeing Jesus (and love) everywhere, as if, suddenly, the dirt was washed from our eyes and we can see! We see more and more.

We actually have a name for this; it's called the "frequency illusion," also known as the Baader-Meinhof phenomenon. It's how our brains work and it's usually just confirmation bias: you start to believe something is more prevalent because you are seeing it more often, even if the frequency hasn't actually increased—that's the illusion part.

For example, you think about getting a new car, a particular make and color, and all of sudden you see them everywhere. That's your brain simply noticing them now that you have given it the information.[18]

Doing "Jesusy" Things

Why not use this amazing brain function to find Jesus in the world today?

This approach encourages me to take a certain perspective on the more controversial stories in the news. I simply ask, *Where is Jesus in this scenario?* What a guide that question is, because you can find Jesus in every scenario—as long as you follow his law of love.

Here's one of my favorite stories, which I share as often as I can because it's a great example of what I think Jesus meant when he said, "I desire mercy, not sacrifice." He wants us not merely to give up stuff, but to get involved. To see another person's circumstance and respond with love, to take action with loving kindness. To be empathetic.

Empathy means we understand how another person is feeling, usually because we have had a similar experience, and if we love like Jesus loved, unconditionally and unhesitatingly, we will act compassionately, because compassion is seeing someone's suffering and wanting to help.

I recently learned that compassion is empathy in action from our Grade 2 social-emotional learning curriculum. Go figure.

Where was I? That's what's so exhilarating about talking about Jesus and love—it's such an inviting rabbit hole. You want to fall into it because it takes you places you never knew existed, let alone considered going to, and all of it makes you feel hopeful, inspired, and motivated. Like this story, the very first one I collected.

In January 2018, Chicago lawyer Jessica Bell posted this story on her Facebook timeline, and it was shared often enough that it made the news and I eventually saw it. I could paraphrase the story, but it really is more powerful in Ms. Bell's words:

> I'm headed home on the CTA Redline and there's a homeless man sitting across from me. He's older, weathered, minding his own business. His feet are so swollen, he's wearing the tattered gym shoes he has with the back folded down, like slip-ons. I don't know how many pairs of socks he's wearing in an attempt to keep his feet warm but there is blood seeping through.

There's another man on the other side of the doors; younger, carrying a satchel and a suitcase, also minding his own business. He's wearing a pair of big black snow boots. They look new; they look expensive; they're built for a Chicago winter.

Quietly, in a "blink and you'll miss it" fashion, the younger man takes off the boots he's wearing and passes them to the old man. He opens his suitcase and gives him a pair of socks as well.

The young man puts on a spare pair of shoes from the suitcase. These shoes are nice, too, but not as nice as the boots. They would have fit the old man just as well, but they were not what he needed.

The younger man tells the old man to try and clean his feet and to make sure he changes into the new socks as soon as he can. Then the young man gets off at 87th.

Those of us who are close enough to see and hear the exchange are floored.

The shoes off his feet.

I love that in a time and place where hate and apathy are rampant, quiet compassion appears without warning. I pray that we all are compelled to do similar... I pray that we never forget that we have always had the power to be a blessing.[19]

We always have the power to be a blessing.

What a Jesusy thing to say. Let's put that on a T-shirt!

So where is Jesus in that scenario? Who is Jesus in that scenario? Is he the homeless man with the bleeding feet? Is he the wealthy businessman with the expensive boots?

Because that's what's really interesting about this story: Jesus was always preaching about those with power and money, shaming them for abusing their power, for not sharing their abundance. Yet on a commuter train in Chicago, we witness Jesus in the world today, present in both the homeless man and the rich man who helped him.

We are, each of us, at any given time, the one needing help or the one providing help. No matter what. No matter who.

Doing "Jesusy" Things

Jesus calls us to radical empathy when he says whatever you do to the lowest of the low, you do to me. Whatever you do. Cut programs or increase funding. Call the police on the guy sitting on a piece of cardboard outside your store, or hand him a cup of coffee and a sandwich. Throw food in the garbage because it spoiled when you didn't get around to eating it, or help make soup for the local mobile food kitchen. Watch as fake police grab a brown-skinned person off the street and drive off with them, or call 9-1-1 about masked armed men driving around your neighborhood.

Whatever you do to them, you do to me, too.

Radical empathy means we find hurting people and we help them. It means tapping into our own experiences, our own suffering, our own losses and betrayals, and find those who are hurting in the same way. It means we join them on their journey.

Jesus showed us the way: Pay attention to the people who are overlooked, whose needs are ignored, who suffer because they are young, old, poor, sick, foreign, differently-abled. Find them, walk with them, speak about them, and more importantly, help them speak for themselves.

I always remind my students to look for the person sitting alone in the cafeteria, to be the brave, kind person who joins them for lunch. "Be kind" is a call to action, not just a catchy slogan on a T-shirt.

In a world that needs more Jesus, we need radical, no-holds-barred, open-to-everyone empathy more than ever.

After all, blessed are those whose feet bleed, for they will know the power and the glory of a new pair of boots.

As Jesus says at the end of his story about the person who stopped to help someone who had been beaten in the street, "Go, and do likewise."[20]

COME AS YOU ARE

It had been a long night
sitting with a friend who was struggling
but a couple of hours ago
another friend had shown up
with coffee and muffins
and afterwards
Jesus had taken his dog for a walk
and passed a church
with a sign out front that read,
"Come as you are!
Everyone welcome!"
so he decided to go to church

He asked Pete to sit outside by the door
and wait for him

Jesus knew he looked tired and untidy
wearing yesterday's now-crumpled clothes
and his long hair not brushed
looked more like he was hungover
than sleepless from worry
but the sign said
"Come as you are"

When he walked through the doors
the man handing out bulletins
frowned
"Good morning," Jesus said

Come as You Are

When he walked up the center aisle
looking for a seat
a woman lighting a big white candle
glanced at him and looked away
"Good morning," Jesus said

When he sat down and started to take off his jacket
the woman behind him tapped his shoulder
and said, "You're sitting in someone else's pew."

When he moved one row ahead
a man came over to him
and said, "Just to let you know
it's Communion Sunday
and we only serve to members of this congregation."

Jesus stood up
looked at the man guarding the communion table
looked at the woman standing beside the candle
looked at the man clutching the bulletins
and walked back down the aisle

After Jesus walked out of the church
Pete greeted him happily
the way he always did
always glad to see Jesus again
after a few minutes or a few hours

As the two headed along the walkway
Jesus stopped and stared at the sign that said
"Come as you are!
Everyone welcome!"

He searched for the asterisk
indicating there were exceptions
he searched for the fine print
that said Members Only

Then he glanced up the street
and saw his two friends walking towards him
the one who had been hurting the night before
waved and said
"Come join us for brunch,"
and Jesus smiled
welcomed the idea of
sitting down and sharing a meal with friends
who loved him as he loved them,
thought
now it's a good morning

4. We Hope It's Not Jesus

ONE OF THE WAYS I think of myself as my father's daughter is picking up his habit, carrying on his routine, of walking the dog first thing in the morning. This was especially meaningful to me when I lived in Vancouver, far away from him, and started walking my dog every morning.

After my first marriage ended, I moved back home to Ontario and lived with my parents for a few years because Dad had been diagnosed with what we now call early-onset dementia. One Sunday morning, the dog and I passed the Anglican church a few minutes before its early service started. (I knew this because it was the church my father liked to attend.) It was a casual service of mostly prayers and hymns and for a long moment I thought about going in and sitting down. A spontaneous decision, spur of the moment. I wondered if I'd be welcomed with my big, quiet Boxer dog, Stella, or if I'd be refused entry. In that hesitation, I kept walking. I guess I assumed the worst; they would say the dog couldn't come in.

The fact I'm still thinking about that moment more than twenty years later says a lot about the pull I felt to go into that quiet, beautiful sanctuary, and about my fear of rejection because of my canine companion.

The event reminds me of the scripture verse, "Do not forget to show hospitality to strangers, for by so doing some people have shown hospitality to angels without knowing it."[21]

Seriously, isn't every dog an angel?

We usually think of hospitality in terms of the "hospitality industry"—restaurants and hotels and resorts. Some areas of the health-care sector are now using the word in terms of "customer service" and referring to patients as "guests."

But what does hospitality mean to a church community, which is supposed to offer sanctuary and welcome and fellowship to all?

When we keep the doors closed, even locked, after worship starts; when we lock the cupboards in our kitchen and put up "instructional" signs telling people what to do and what not do, what are we telling the community around us? What kind of welcome can they expect from us?

If hospitality is the center of our faith, what is it supposed to look like?

Hospitality is about meeting the stranger and welcoming them into our midst without worrying if they can pay you back or if their boots are dirty. Hospitality doesn't even require a belief in God; it's simply the act of welcoming whomever comes through the door, no questions asked. There is no application to fill out so we can determine if they would be a good fit for us. Hospitality is about opening our space to whomever needs time, rest, nurture, and support. And that space is as much about our heart as it is about our sanctuary or our home.

I love this story shared by Peter J. Gomes in his book *The Scandalous Gospel of Jesus*:

> I was preparing to preach as a guest minister in a very posh church, and just as the rector and I were about to proceed to our prayers before the service, a wildly disoriented young man burst into the room. He spoke loudly but nonsensically, seemingly either "on" or "off" something. Whatever it was, though, his erratic behavior was familiar to the rector, who treated him with enormous but firm courtesy and let the little tantrum run its course. The intruder left as abruptly as he had arrived, and while I was shaken, the rector was not, and was clearly used to such interruptions. As we pulled ourselves together, his thoughtful comment was, "I keep hoping it isn't Jesus."[22]

We Hope It's Not Jesus

I keep hoping it isn't Jesus.

And what about us? Jesus says, "Truly I tell you, whatever you did for one of the least of these brothers and sisters of mine, you did for me…"[23] So if it had been us in the story, why would we hope it wasn't Jesus? Because we didn't welcome the distraught man just as he was and try to figure out what he needed? Because we don't do everything we possibly can to welcome the stranger—in whatever state they arrive—and give them sanctuary? Because we worry more about carpets and cups, pews and plates getting dirty or broken or just plain used than we do about what people really need—food and shelter, for example?

Jesus showed us who we should welcome, and it isn't just the ones who pre-purchased tickets in the box seats with their credit cards, and it isn't just the ones who pull up to the door for the valet parking; it isn't just the ones who sit at the head table and have their glasses refilled without asking, and it isn't the ones who have the ear of the chairman or the senator.

Jesus wants us to show hospitality to everyone, to those who need it but can't ask for it as well as to those who expect it, or who believe they have earned it.

"Jesus did not preach from a place of rigid binaries and judgments but from a place of continual becoming," says California pastor Molly Phinney Baskette "He befriended outcasts and lived on the margins of society while staying in relationship with wealthy and powerful people, some of whom became patrons and disciples."[24]

Jesus asks us to welcome "the least" among us[25] yet not to the exclusion of those who have the most. People with an abundance of money and stuff may be "poor in spirit"[26] or seeking Jesus with a genuine desire to help others.

Hence Jesus' call for us to show hospitality to everyone, especially to the poor, the sick, the disabled, the broken-hearted. The quiet and the awkward and the non-verbal. To the weary and the dirty, to the ones who act erratically, and even to the ones who might pass out as soon as they get to a pew—maybe they're not drunk; maybe they just feel safe enough to rest.

Those people might be Jesus.

Is it just me or do hospitality and justice have a lot in common? The basic idea of justice is respect, dignity, and the protection of rights and opportunities for all.[27] The basic idea, and expectation, of hospitality is welcome everyone.

That means hospitality is love in action (as in, love your neighbor). Love is hospitality is justice. We are called to love and to do justice. We are called to love and to show hospitality to others. We are called to love and do justice and welcome strangers—foreigners, refugees, asylum seekers, every person—no matter who they are and where they come from, no matter how much baggage they are lugging. Love is justice is hospitality.

Sister Joan Chittister said, "Hospitality is the way we turn a prejudiced world around, one heart at a time."[28]

So knowing love is an action we take, what does this mean?

It means, for example, we go to the airport and look for asylum seekers coming off planes because we're going to offer hospitality, aren't we? They're sent to the city's intake office, which manages emergency shelters, but those shelters are already filled. There is no room at the inn, so these peace and freedom seekers are forced to sleep on downtown streets because there is no welcome for them.

If we knew one of them was Jesus, how would we help? What would we offer?

Love in action means we see the hundreds of people who live in tent cities and who, in the midst of torrential rain and thunderstorms, have nowhere safe to go. In response, comfort centers might be opened for people dealing with flooding and power outages. But will strangers living in tents be welcomed too, those with no electricity, no basements to flood. Do they count?

If we knew one of them was Jesus, how would we help? What would we offer?

As one shelter posted on social media in the middle of a rainstorm, "Tents are not safe shelter and they are not homes. Housing is a human right."

That's justice and hospitality rolled into one.

We Hope It's Not Jesus

First, the issue of adequate housing and shelter for everyone is always an issue. It's part of human reality and can't be ignored because it's about dignity for all human beings, regardless of their struggles.

Second, our climate is changing, so weather events are getting more severe, more dangerous. In the face of natural disasters, our response to the least among us is a matter of justice and hospitality.

We who live with abundance are called to help those who have less and need more. As the 13th-century Christian mystic Mechtild of Magdeburg said, "Hospitality is an essential spiritual practice." Even more, like the prophets before him, Jesus calls us to love, to do justice, to live with kindness and mercy. We are called to welcome the stranger, the foreigner, the refugee, the asylum seeker, and to say, "I have space for you. Come with me. I will take care you. Don't be afraid. Put down your burdens and rest with me. You are safe. I will give you shelter."

All of which sounds very Jesusy, doesn't it? But that's who we're supposed to sound like. No one should be "least" among us since justice means fairness.

Everyone has a safe place to live.

Everyone can find a bed in a shelter.

Everyone is welcome at a comfort center.

The needs of everyone are met without conditions, without judgment.

Because you never know if Jesus is one of them.

RED TAPE

Jesus sits on the concrete steps
next to a sign that reads

FREE MEALS
FREE BEDS
FREE SHOWERS

the heavy wooden doors of the building behind him
are wide open

as he leans on his bent knees,
a shadow falls across him
and Jesus shades his eyes as he looks up
at the by-law officer standing on the sidewalk in front of him

"Did you get a permit for this?" he asks
jerking his thumb at the sign

Jesus sighs
"Blessed are those who are poor
but welcome others with grace and humility."

the by-law officer hands him a ticket

as he leans on his bent knees
a shadow falls across him
and Jesus shades his eyes as he looks up
at the municipal clerk standing on the sidewalk in front of him

Red Tape

"You're not zoned for this," she says
kicking at the sign with her right shoe

Jesus sighs
"Blessed are those who are starved for justice
but don't talk about their struggles."

the municipal officer hands him a notice of violation

as he leans on his bent knees
a shadow falls across him
and Jesus shades his eyes as he looks up
at the chair of the church board standing on the sidewalk

"We didn't bring this to the congregation for a vote," he says
poking a finger at the sign

Jesus sighs
"Blessed are those who are merciful
and welcome strangers into their space."

the chair of the board hands him a copy of the church manual

as he leans on his bent knees
a shadow falls across him
and Jesus shades his eyes as he looks up
at the member of the community council standing on the sidewalk

"We don't want these people in our neighborhood," she says
and draws a line across the sign with a large black marker

Jesus sighs
"Blessed are those who are persecuted
but continue to love their neighbor."

the member of the community council hands him a petition

Jesus in the World Today

Jesus looks at the list of names
on the petition
then puts a hand on each corner
and rips the paper right down the center

"Blessed are the peace seekers,"
he says
standing up
his long shadow falling over the stairs
and right up to the doors behind him
"for they are not afraid to do the right thing."

as he looks at the bylaw officer and the municipal clerk,
the chair of the church board and the member of the community council,
he shades his eyes

the heat of the afternoon sun burns into
the scar on his palm
reminding him of the days when he
needed a good meal and a soft bed and a long, hot shower
and he says,
"Blessed are those who see this sign
and walk up these steps
without knowing what is inside that building
but having faith
it speaks the truth
and shows the way
and their life is worth
the baking of bread
and the making of a bed
and the water being poured out
as if loving your neighbor
was as easy
and expected
as that."

5. When Hope Becomes Subversive

IF WE ARE TO truly understand Jesus, what he came to accomplish and what he still asks us to accomplish, we have to sit with our discomfort with some of the words that describe him:

>Prophetic
>Revolutionary
>Progressive
>Radical
>Subversive

The word subversive comes from Latin: *Sub* means from below and *vertere* means to turn. So to subvert means to turn things upside-down.

Jesus was all about turning things upside down, but he didn't just toss tables in the temple; he overturned cultural norms, challenged the authorities, undermined the establishment, and generally shook everything up. He was a troublemaker, a dissident, a thorn in the side of the establishment.

The Establishment. The System. The People with All the Power Who Want to Maintain the Status Quo and Who Hate People Like Jesus.

Religious leaders considered Jesus dangerous and that's how they justified killing him. He was going to draw the attention of the Romans, who responded to those who challenged them with violence and brutal repression, and that would not go well for the people with power and influence.

They killed him because they needed to maintain "the System." As it was then, and as it is now.

What do I mean by "the System" as we know it today? It's patriarchy. It's white supremacy. It's racism. It's misogyny. It's transphobia. It's colonization. It's the way we do things that oppresses women, particularly women of color, Black people, Indigenous people, queer and non-binary people, transgender people, disabled people, people living in poverty, and people living with addictions and mental health issues.

The prejudices and negative stereotypes that flow from these identities have existed from the beginnings of our faith. Paul was persecuted because he wrote and preached relentlessly about how everyone is one, or equal, in Christ, a message the Roman authorities would have considered a declaration of resistance. After Christianity was given the stamp of approval by the Roman emperor Constantine, Mary Magdalene was branded a prostitute by Pope Gregory in 591 CE, as a way to diminish the power and influence of the first person who witnessed Jesus' appearance days after his death. Both of these apostles, and others like them, really bugged the People with All the Power Who Want to Maintain the Status Quo and Who Hate People Like Jesus.

For some people today, terms like "white privilege" and "colonization," and talk of creating a whole new system (built on a foundation other than white privilege and colonization, racism and misogyny), are distressing and very discomfiting. People are suspicious of change and fear they will be on the losing end because they believe they have something to lose—money, property, influence. They want to know what's so bad about the way things are now, anyway? It's worked for years, centuries, generations.

Worked for some people, yes.

So what happened to following the man we describe with such words as

Prophetic
Revolutionary
Progressive
Radical
Subversive

Ever since Jesus walked around telling people to love one another and to give each other the shirt off their back, and maybe their coat, too, since they likely have three more hanging in their closet at home, we have been challenged by—and either embraced or resisted—the idea that there is a new way to do things based on a new truth. A way that is fair, inclusive, peaceful, and merciful. A way that welcomes everyone, no matter who they are.

With his message and his mission, Jesus hoped to change a system, a way of doing things, that excluded so many, that was unfair and harmful to so many. He hoped to create a new way, a different system based on the re-distribution of wealth and property, and the de-construction of our institutions in order to release people—all people—from the prisons of poverty, prejudice, and oppression. He wanted to free not only bodies, but minds and hearts.

That was the point of Jesus' ministry and teachings: to free people from the captivity of fear and self-interest, and from the captivity of the structures and systems that diminish and destroy lives. In the first century, Jesus stood in the temple, amongst the money changers and people selling birds and animals for sacrifice, and shouted, "My house shall be called a house of prayer for all the nations—but you have made it a den of robbers."[29] Selling animals at the temple was accepted practice but Jesus objected to the way the money changers and sellers jacked their prices for travelers and poor locals. In the twenty-first century, Jesus could stand on the steps of Parliament or Congress, on the steps of a church espousing Christian nationalism,[30] and shout, "This house should be considered a house of peace for all the nations—but you are turning it into a place of liars and cheaters and thieves."

Yet if he did that today, he would be condemned as disruptive, disrespectful, not law-abiding. We are still looking for the nice, polite do-gooder in the stories of a troublemaker who wanted to subvert the world as we know it.

Who do you say I am?

Jesus is the one who healed people on the Sabbath, an act that was against the religious laws of the time. When the Pharisees challenged him and refused to tell him why it was wrong to do good, to save a life on the Sabbath, he was angry at their hypocrisy and also disappointed because they lacked compassion.

In the twenty-first century, Jesus would stand on the steps of a hospital where they hand a widowed parent a bill for the final days of his wife's life, or at the doors of a government office where they are refusing to cover the cost of a drug to treat a teenager's cancer.

Who do you say I am?

Jesus is not "the System." He is not "the Establishment." He definitely is not "the Empire." He is not the government or the politicians, the bankers or the corporate CEOs. He is not a white savior wearing a red ball cap.

He is the rebel, the prophet, the revolutionary, the subverter.

The upside-down bringer of the good news of justice and mercy.

The upside-down blesser of those whom the system wants to ignore, outlaw, eradicate—the same people we are called to serve, to love, to help, to work alongside: those who are despairing because the system keeps them down; those who are hungry and thirsty for fairness and justice; those who mourn the deaths of people of color; those who are non-binary and persecuted for their bravery and authenticity; those who struggle with addiction and/or mental health issues, and their families trying to support and heal them; and those who are rounded up and taken to detention centers without being charged, without being able to contact their family.

Jesus blessed those who need hope. Jesus asks us to serve those who need hope.

Today, he may even ask us to fight, with nonviolent means, for those who need hope.

Hope is found in the eyes and ears of those who are willing to listen and to observe, no matter how uncomfortable what we hear and see makes us. Hope is found in the hearts and minds of those whose people have suffered because of "the System," and who themselves suffer—yet turn again and again to Jesus for guidance, for strength, for courage, for peace, for acceptance. For a new way and a new truth.

Hope is found in people like Indigenous author Kaitlin B. Curtice, a Christian and a citizen of the Potawatomi nation, who writes the following in her book *Native: Identity, Belonging, and Rediscovering God*: "The books I am writing and the words I am speaking are for the purpose of bringing peace"; and "I believe toxic systems will crumble beneath the glorious weight of world-rattling, inclusive joy—but to get there, the church has a lot of work to do."[31]

Peace. Joy. That's what she's seeking. That's the spirit she's bringing to her work and to the church, to God. Peace and joy. That's her prayer for all nations.

How subversive. Then again, peace and joy are nonviolent acts of resistance.

This is the edge we stand on at the end of the first quarter of the twenty-first century. This is the turning point for more than 2,000 years of Christianity. This is the potential to achieve our purpose as Christians: to love one another as Jesus loved us, the commandment he gave in the hours before his death. He could have said so many other things, but he said the one thing that covers it all: Love one another.

This is what Jesus lived and died for—the destruction of systems that oppress and demean and exclude, and the rising up of a new way of co-existing and encouraging where peace, love, and hope are the foundation stones, where everyone is equal and worthy and welcome. In all the nations.

And if that's what it means to be subversive, so be it.

THE EMPIRE

Jesus looked around
at the men in robes
at the armored police
at the crowd chanting

Why does all of this seem so familiar?
is this the first century or the twenty-first?
he wondered

What can I say now that I haven't said
a thousand times before?

I don't even know where to begin anymore
I don't even know where to go first
who to help next
how to make sense of any of this

Why can't there be more of me?
he wondered

Then he looked at the gathered crowd
at the faces of
those living in poverty whose spirit is abundant
those who are grieving and comforting each other
the gentle ones who are shouting and waving their hand-drawn signs
the people preparing the feast of justice and fairness
the angels of mercy who rush in seeking survivors
the pure in heart whose eyes shine with the light of hope
the peacemakers who work on behalf of the children
the wronged and the victimized, the mistreated and the misgendered

The Empire

the profiled and the detained
those ignored and discounted, harassed and harmed
by those who think they speak words of virtue and morality
by those who lie and manipulate and cheat
by those who think war is righteous

"Blessed are you," he cried out
"when people insult you
and persecute you
and discredit you through misinformation
because you believe in

love
and acceptance
peace
and mercy
truth
freedom
and the common good."

The crowd roared
as Jesus raised his arms
in blessing
light piercing
the wounds in his hands
shining on the faces of those
who could be more of him

if only
the empire wasn't watching
and taking notes
taking aim
and firing
from its safe distance
barricaded
behind desks

Jesus in the World Today

behind fences
behind the walls they build
a bit higher
every time

THOSE PEOPLE

Jesus—may I call you Jesus?—
you seem like a man in need.
I mean,
you're a little—
dusty—
and you look tired.
Are you getting enough sleep, Jesus?
You seem like a man
with a lot on his mind.

So here's the thing, Jesus—
I can help with that.
I've got just what you need
to take all your worries away.
I can help you get a little security,
some peace of mind,
maybe even a new life.
Imagine!
No more worrying
about having enough money
or where your next meal is coming from
or how to pay for a new pair of shoes—
and—may I speak frankly, Jesus? -
you're in need of a new pair of shoes
and that coat's a little ragged
and your shirt looks like it's been
through the wash
a few too many times -
ha ha, you know what I mean!

Jesus in the World Today

But seriously,
Jesus,
you can buy a whole new wardrobe
just step into my office
where we can talk more comfortably
because you seem a little distracted
by those people over there.

Those people –
are they upsetting you, Jesus?
I can make a call, I've done it before
Are those people bothering you, Jesus?
Protestors, I tell you,
always complaining about something,
always demanding justice for someone,
nothing's ever right with them.
Now they want to change the system.
If it ain't broke, don't fix it, amiright, Jesus?

The system's fine,
it's those people who are the problem.
Get a job, I keep saying to them,
get out of my neighborhood,
you're blocking traffic,
I keep saying to those people.

Just between you and me, Jesus—
because you look like a man
who works for a living,
those are the hands of a man
willing to make sacrifices
for what he believes in—
let me tell you,
they just need to get a job, you know?
Work ten hours a day like the rest of us
instead of standing around holding signs
and shouting at good people who are just trying do their jobs.

Those People

If those people are upsetting you, Jesus,
I can make that phone call, just say the word.
Out of sight, out of mind—
ha ha –

But seriously,
come into my office
and let's talk about what you want to achieve
what you see as your purpose in life.
The paperwork's a breeze,
we can have you set up by the end of the day—
hey, Jesus,
where are you going?
What are you doing?

Hey, man, was it necessary
to flip that table
on your way out the door?

6. What If?

IMAGINE SOMEONE BORN INTO a humble family, with only a bit of fanfare—a simple announcement, people in the community excited when they hear about the good news, a few nice gifts. This person grows up on the lowdown, not making waves, not making headlines, until as a young adult this person suddenly becomes someone who gets everyone's attention.

This unknown person is thrown into the spotlight. Wherever this person goes people are following, shouting questions, taking photos. Over time, this person starts to get bad press, certain people, people with power, start to run this person down, mocking and denigrating choices and statements, trying to get them in trouble.

Yet this person is making an impact on people's lives. This person is bringing hope to people from certain segments of society—suddenly, others are noticing them, bringing attention to their plight, demanding answers and change.

The people with power don't like it. They don't like the following this person has; they don't like that this person is more popular than they are, and makes them look out of touch and elitist. They don't like that this person is going to name names.

Perhaps they arrange to have this person taken out.

Yet after this person dies their legacy grows stronger, takes on a life of its own. This person's words and actions continue to impact and influence others for decades, for generations, all over the world. This person is immortalized and revered for the good deeds and goodness they displayed, particularly in the latter part of their short life. Everyone knows this person's life, and no one will ever forget.

Sounds like Jesus, right?

Except I'm talking about Princess Diana.

Stay with me: While Lady Diana Spencer wasn't born in a stable, she was minor aristocracy so, in her context, suddenly becoming the fiancée of the future king of England was a big leap from obscurity to instant fame. She was an unknown young woman working as a nursery teacher's assistant suddenly thrust into the public limelight, into intense and relentless scrutiny because she was born into a destiny she did not choose.

She was the "virgin" who was the appropriate choice to become the wife of the future king, a decision apparently made by her grandmother and by his grandmother, two friends looking out for the future of the monarchy.

Diana had supporters and followers, and eventually, detractors. Things got quite nasty for her, particularly after she and Charles divorced. The paparazzi took away all her privacy. Her influence seemed to threaten the royal status quo. Yet at the same time she battled with those in power who wanted to silence her, what else was she doing? Visiting men dying of AIDS at a time when the world was terrified of AIDS.

What was her last project before she died? Calling for the eradication of the use of landmines, a call famously illustrated by her 1997 walk through a field in Angola that had been cleared of landmines.

Diana had realized she could use her wealth and influence, her public identity, to change the world (sadly, landmines are still in use today).

On the 20th anniversary of her death in 2017, I watched a long documentary about Princess Diana's life and death. One of the theories about her death is that she was about to name names, outing those involved in making, distributing, and profiting from the use of land mines, an exposé that would have rocked the world in which she lived: with the wealthy and the influential, with millionaire businesspeople, politicians, and aristocrats. The documentary claimed she had to die because she was going to shake things up. And yet she was already shaking things up; she was already opening people's eyes to compassion and kindness, to corruption and warmongering.

The response to her death? She was instantly immortalized as the "People's Princess."

My intention with this idea, this comparison between Jesus and Diana, isn't to shock and upset you but instead to encourage you to think and consider what it might mean. What if we are *all* manifestations of God, of good, of Love?

I believe each of us has something special we do: the ability to perform "miracles," or create "healing," or to "proclaim," but we don't know it. Or we are desperately afraid of our ability.

Author Marianne Williamson said, "Our deepest fear is not that we are inadequate. Our deepest fear is that we are powerful beyond measure. It is our light, not our darkness that most frightens us." She added, "Your playing small does not serve the world."[32]

After all, a miracle is simply doing something that seemed impossible—like taking care of a loved one with a chronic illness or organizing a group of people to create and maintain a community garden. Healing doesn't mean curing an illness but rather making someone feel whole again by accepting them exactly as they are, where they are, no matter what they do, or cannot do. Proclaiming doesn't mean standing on a street corner shouting scripture at people, it means speaking of and acting out of love and compassion, justice and mercy.

Perhaps perceiving that our talents and skills can help others is all the proof we need in order to know that we are manifestations of God, of good, of Love, but still we stubbornly choose to deny our destiny.

Jesus was one of us. Yet over time, with the way stories are told and retold and changed, and given how legends are created and imprinted on humans, Jesus became the one and only manifestation. So, what if we're doing not only ourselves but also Jesus a huge disservice by thinking so small, by limiting ourselves so much? What if we're keeping ourselves, and thus our potential as humans, in a very small box? Our playing small does not serve the world.

Remember the story of John the Baptist dunking people in the river in order to wash them clean and prepare them for the arrival of the Messiah. And when that Messiah—who happened to be John's cousin—showed up? Jesus wanted John to baptize him like everybody else.

Because Jesus was one of them, and he is one of us.

And what happened to Jesus during his baptism? The Spirit showed up.

Listen, I hope you're familiar with the feeling you get when what you're doing is the right thing for you. As in, The Right Thing. It's an amazing feeling of grace and joy. A quiet "woo hoo" whispered by your inner voice. We feel energized, elated; we feel like we are doing our thing, what is meant for us to do. Sometimes, we're so happy, we cry.

That's how we, too, can experience the moment that Jesus did. The Spirit—the holy, divine energy of the universe, of the eons, the energy that infused Jesus—is here for us as well and can inspire and empower us as it inspired and empowered Jesus.

If we are ignited by the same Spirit Jesus possessed, are we not manifestations of that same source, too? Might this be what God wanted all along?

But because we fear what we don't know, what we can't see and prove; because we don't want to fail or look foolish; because we worry that we're wrong or not worthy, we resist the idea that each of us is a divine manifestation of God. It's so much easier to put it all on one person. That way we don't really have to check our own behavior. We don't have to walk around like we are here for a very specific purpose (which, to be clear, is to love). We don't have to act and speak in ways that uphold the teachings of Jesus: teaching about compassion, mercy, justice, hope, peace, inclusion, and dignity.

All of which he died for.

The teachings Princess Diana died for.

The teachings countless others since the first century died and will continue to die for.

The teachings from Jesus' great declarations known as "the Beatitudes": Blessed are the poor in spirit, blessed are those who mourn, blessed are the meek, blessed are those who hunger and thirst for righteousness, blessed are the merciful, blessed are the pure in heart, blessed are the peacemakers.

Princess Diana's public work was a reflection of the Beatitudes; she was merciful and kind, she fought to right wrongs, she strived to create peace. Even as she struggled with privilege and fame, paparazzi and notoriety.

Wherever we find Jesus, we find ourselves.

Until we start believing that we are each a manifestation of God—of love—just like Jesus was, we will leave it up to a few people who have had their destiny thrust upon them to do all the work of changing this world for the better.

POLITICALLY MOTIVATED

On an after-supper walk
the end-of-summer air twilight and cooling
Jesus pauses as his dog stops to sniff a tree

a person strolls up the sidewalk
and Jesus greets them as they pass by
"Nice evening."

the person nods then halts mid-stride
"You look familiar," they say
"Are you running in the election?"

Jesus shakes his head
"No, I'm not. I'm not really into politics."

"Who is these days?" the person says
"It's just the same old crap.
Politicians saying whatever it takes to get elected.
Nothing ever changes.
I mean, look around.
The rich are richer, the poor are poorer."

the dog turns away from the tree
and sniffs the person's shoes
the person pats his head

"What matters to a dog? Food, naps and walks, right?
To love and be loved in return.
And what is love
if not taking care of each other?

Jesus in the World Today

Every person deserves food and water,
a place to live,
the proper clothes for winter.
Don't get me started about health care!
And prisons—
do you know Indigenous people
account for thirty per cent of incarcerations?"

Jesus lifts his eyebrows
"You seem pretty passionate about these issues.
Why aren't you running in the election?"

The person snorts
"No one would vote for a person like me."

Jesus smiles
"Good news!
There are people who will listen to your message.
There are people who will follow you.
Sometimes
you can shake up the system from outside the system."

the person laughs
"Yeah, right. Name one person who has done that."

Jesus raises his hand

"Oh, man, that's quite a scar on your palm.
What happened to you?"

Jesus lowers his hand
"I tried to change the system."

"See? That's what I'm talking about.
They crucify you, don't they?
They don't want to help people,

they don't want to change the system.
The world is run by CEOs, man,
who don't care about the poor and hungry,
the broken-hearted and the peaceful protestors."

"But you do," Jesus says, "and that's what matters.
You care about people here and now,
in this world, in this life.
And you never know who might be listening,
who you might inspire, even if you don't see it today.
Even the smallest gesture can reap a large reward."

the dog nudges the person's fingers with his nose

"Yeah, sure. Well, nice talking to you.
That's a good dog you got there.
See you around."

the person walks away
Jesus sighs
the dog sits down

"I don't think he's convinced, Pete.
Wanna walk to the lake?
There's always people hanging out on the shore."

the dog stands up and wags his tail
the only word he ever recognizes is
walk

7. Jesus Is Political

WHAT DOES IT MEAN to be political?

First, it can simply mean that something is relevant to politics, that it has political origins, implications, or effects; that it is a topic of public concern. On the other hand, it's often used dismissively to undermine or even discredit others, as when people speak about "political competition" or "political protest," or when claiming a previously routine matter "has become very political."

We hear this a lot: Don't be political. A celebrity or sports star should "stay out of politics." People comment on social media posts, "I don't follow you for the politics."

We hear: The church shouldn't be political.

We even hear that Jesus wasn't political.

Seriously? Have you read the gospels?

You can't consider someone's life's work "the upside-down gospel" or refer to him as "radical" and not know his life's work was deeply political.

Jesus blesses the poor and tells the rich they will face troubles. He has harsh words for leaders of nations when they fail to care for the needy. Jesus is deeply concerned about how we treat the poor, which is a political issue because we vote for people who make decisions about the poor and the vulnerable on our behalf.

Jesus' work and life is also political because he commanded us to love our neighbors as he loved us, so how we vote is our love in action, our love in public.

Yep, love is political.

Jesus Is Political

Let's be honest. What makes following Jesus (which means voting in a way that supports the actual teachings of Jesus) so hard is that he calls us to think about others and to put others' needs before our own. Following Jesus means putting our faith before platform and policy. Following Jesus requires us to love our neighbors as Jesus loved us. That's unconditional love. Love without exceptions. Love without limits. Love without borders.

Some people like to vote for "law and order," but what exactly is the law we are asked to vote for? Is it the law of love? Is it a law that demands we love our neighbor? *And* our enemy? Is it a love that wants us to turn the other cheek or give the shirt off our back? Honestly, you have ten more shirts in your closet, don't you? If the pandemic taught those of us living an abundant life anything, it's that we have way more socks and underwear and coats and shirts than we truly need.

The politics of fear and scarcity pushes us to worry that if we give someone our coat and shirt, they'll ask for more and suddenly we won't have anything. So we hoard our abundance and feel safe with all our stuff, without realizing that we only really need one shirt, one coat, and one pair of shoes. The rest is retail therapy.

Writing in *Sojourners* magazine, Rev. Dr. Mark Sandlin, with the Presbyterian Church (USA), created a list of ten political things you can't do if you follow Jesus. Here are five of them:

1. Favor the rich over the poor
2. Advocate for war
3. Let people go hungry
4. Limit the rights of a select group of people
5. Turn away immigrants[33]

Funny how "taking care of each other" and "loving your neighbor"—as Jesus taught us to do—suddenly becomes wrong and detrimental when we talk politics.

Pastor Andy Stanley in Atlanta, Georgia, put it this way: "It was the teachings of Jesus, not our political parties, that laid the groundwork for our modern sense of justice and fairness and dignity of every single individual."[34]

Given that the world as we know it, the world of Western culture, has been in existence since the fourth century of the Common Era, and is supposed to be based on the teachings of Jesus—the main focus of which is love—we have done a rather poor job of

- not going to war
- welcoming immigrants and migrants and refugees
- feeding the hungry and supporting the poor
- embracing diversity and inclusivity.

In fact, we've done almost everything in complete opposition to the teachings that are supposedly the foundation of Western civilization. Just look at slavery, and residential schools.

No wonder Jesus weeps.

This is why I always say the world needs more Jesus. We know what Jesus wants us to do, we just choose not to do it.

What makes Jesus political in the twenty-first century?

His call for unity.

This is not a new call; it's right there in the Gospel of John. But given the current trends of the politics of division and the politics of fear, obviously we really, really need to hear it again—or truly hear it for the first time.

After his last Passover meal, Jesus prayed, "I have given them the glory that you gave me, that *they may be one as we are one*—I in them and you in me—so that they may be brought to complete unity."[35]

That they may be one. Unified. Unified by the commandment to love one another, by Jesus' love for them—by the love of God.

All for love, love for all. Let's put *that* on a T-shirt!

This prayer was Jesus' final petition to God on behalf of the disciples—that they may remain unified as they head out into the world to share his message, and to face everything he figured awaited them, including rejection and violence. It doesn't take much to divide people; we disagree, give up, cut ties, take our toys and go home over small petty things, let alone big, actually important issues.

Jesus also prays for the unity of future generations, those who might hear about his teachings through his followers. Basically, Jesus asked for unity for everyone and forever. He prays for unity among those who hear his blessings and his final commandment, who learn about his support of the poor and hungry, the persecuted and oppressed, the hurt and the broken; all those people who are pushed down, pushed aside, ignored, persecuted and oppressed by an empire. Jesus calls us to be united in our support of those who are deserted by the government and by politicians, who are persecuted and blamed as the reason why we need divisions and why we need to fear.

And yet, for hundreds and hundreds of years, when we hear Jesus' calls for unity, when we hear his prayer for his followers, for us Christians, for all of us who believe because of the belief and bravery and persistence of the disciples, when we hear Jesus' call to be unified by his commandment to love one another—and our enemy—we respond with the politics of division, fear, and privilege.

Or we don't respond at all.

And that, my friends, is why Jesus is political.

WHERE ARE YOU?

Jesus says

I am in Ethiopia Sudan Somalia
the Democratic Republic of Congo
I am in Yemen Afghanistan
I am in Gaza and the West Bank

I am in the bombed-out hospitals
the overcrowded refugee camps
the rubble of apartment buildings
the mass graves
the crowds waiting for food supplies
the line of cars carts donkeys
on the only road through the only safe zone

I am where
fighting and flooding
drought and disease
malnutrition and famine
financial crisis and economic collapse
are killing children
and mothers and grandparents

Where are you?

Jesus says

I know, I know
there is enough going on in your own country
in your own life

Where Are You?

the news is depressing
you have enough to worry about
your kids and bills to pay
inflation and the high cost of living
how to pay for food gas medicine
cars clothes phones take-out

but when
Russia invaded Ukraine
suddenly you were
praying and protesting
lamenting and loudly declaring the war
unjust and illegal
wearing blue and yellow
for a country you wouldn't find on a map
the day before

Where were you when
freedoms (and people) disappeared in Syria?

Where were you when
Boko Haram abducted school children in Nigeria?

Where were you when
China forced Uyghurs into internment camps?

Where are you when
girls study in a secret, hidden school in Afghanistan?

Where are you when
bombs are dropped on hospitals and schools
killing Palestinians needing care and shelter?

Where are you when
trucks carrying food water and medicine
are blocked from entering Gaza?

Jesus in the World Today

Where are you when
children are starving to death?

Where are you when
the word genocide is spoken
into a chasm of silence
and the truth is twisted into lies
and law

Where are you when world leaders
talk and dither and wring their hands
do nothing to help
do not hold accountable
just hold back aid

Where are your prayers and laments
your protests and declarations
when disease sweeps through a refugee camp?
when famine fills graves?
when snipers shoot pregnant women?
when blood runs in the ancient dust?

I am here
I was there
I am wherever
innocent victims
of ego, power and greed
are
shot
beaten
kidnapped
attacked
invaded
bombed
terrorized

Where Are You?

The scars in my palms
throb
as fear and courage
despair and outrage
sorrow and mercy
course through my veins

The scars in my palms
throb
against the forehead of the dying
so they know they are beloved
by me
even though the world has ignored them

The scars in my palms
throb
as I raise them against
the war
the warriors
the police
the policies

I am here
I am there
I am everywhere
love cries out
in pain
in suffering

in the heartbeat and the breath
in the blood and the bones
of everyone beloved by me

I am here

Where are you?

THE SHORES OF SABRATHA

(June 2023)

Jesus leaned against one of the pillars
amid the ruins of the Temple of Isis
watching a fishing trawler
move away from the shore of Sabratha

even from a distance
he could tell the boat was carrying
too many humans

This is not what I meant
when I said
I will make you fishers of people

He knew who was crammed on that boat
sailing from Libya to Italy
refugees and migrants
Pakistanis and Egyptians, Syrians and Afghans
people already displaced from their homelands

people willing to do anything to escape
war persecution poverty
disease and disaster and despair

people who see their only hope
in paying what little money they have
to climb aboard a crowded boat
and head out to sea

The Shores of Sabratha

willing to risk their lives
for a better life in Europe
willing to risk their lives
for an unwelcomed arrival
willing to risk their lives
because they believe they are
worth the risk

Watching the rusted blue-painted trawler
motor through the white-tipped waves
under the hot shining sun
Jesus had a bad feeling about this

Didn't everyone? he wondered
How could this be anything but
another disaster waiting to happen?
A story told again and again
a story told so many times
the world no longer paid attention
to a boat full of desperate human beings
and not enough fuel
trying to cross a sea
on nothing but the promise the illusion
of freedom

He rubbed his face
he couldn't just sit here and watch
knowing what was going to happen
he couldn't turn away and ignore it

the rest of the world might be able to
but he was not of this world

Jesus in the World Today

These were not rich men trying to get into Heaven
by seeing how far how high how deep
their money could take them
these were his Muslim siblings
his cousins in faith
his companions on this journey
of mercy and justice

Yet his presence on that boat
would not change their lives now

by the time they boarded
his work had failed
his words had fallen on hardened ground
his example had been rejected
all he could offer was
peace
and his witness to their suffering

He couldn't help himself
he jumped up and ran down the dirt path
over the rocks
towards the water
towards the boat

as the news tuned out another story about
the poor and the desperate
and tuned into the futile attempt to rescue
the rich from themselves

8. Blessed Are the Fixers

A COUPLE OF SUMMERS ago, I had the opportunity to provide pulpit supply for ten weeks. Ten weeks! That meant I could do a deep dive into my favorite subject: Love. I decided to do a sermon series called "Summer of Love" and each Sunday my sermon focused on a different sub-category of Love: concepts like mercy, hospitality, inclusion, forgiveness, healing, peace, and justice.

I discovered that writing about justice is the same as writing about climate change, refugees, accessibility, or housing. Justice is a broad, deep, and multi-faceted subject that is part of everything, including climate change, refugees, accessibility, and housing. Justice plays a part, or doesn't play a part, in everything we say and do, don't say and don't do, as individuals, as a community, as a province or state, and as a nation. And, from a Jesusy point of view, as humanity.

Justice must be done, it must be called out, so I found courage in the words of American pastor Michael Eric Dyson: "Justice is what love sounds like when it speaks in public."[36] I'm writing and speaking about Jesus, and as we know, Jesus and justice go hand-in-hand, so if you follow Jesus, then justice is your thing, because it was very much his thing.

But like love, justice is a big thing. And the biggest stumbling block for me are the many examples of injustice in the world.

My default understanding of how we have lived the Christian faith is that we have not done a good job of following Jesus, of doing what he wanted us to do. He was killed because he challenged the status quo by asking us to take care of those who couldn't take care of themselves, and to stop buying so many sandals and wanting a bigger house. He challenged those with power and money and influence to share those things with others who had less—but because they had power and money and influence, they were able to get him killed and thus keep their jobs, and build a sandal closet, and buy a bigger house.

It doesn't seem like much has changed.

Where do we even start to talk about that?

When it came to writing my sermon that summer, I very quickly got bogged down thinking about all the ways we don't do justice or mercy or reconciliation. I couldn't filter any of it out and I couldn't find a focus. By the end of the morning, I found myself tangled up and frustrated and feeling overwhelmed. I took a break and ate lunch, but of course my brain kept buzzing and spinning like a fly caught inside a window frame. I came up with a new way to write the sermon and was just heading back to my computer when my best friend, Sarah, called.

I asked if I could call her back later because I had to rewrite my sermon on justice, and it was hard and …

Thirty minutes later, I hung up the phone and dashed upstairs to write down our conversation because it was all about justice.

We all need one friend who is a gentle teacher, who reminds us to breathe, then tells us what we didn't know we needed to hear. Like Jesus did.

Sarah and I have been friends since high school but have lived a thousand miles apart for nearly twenty years. Before that, we lived much closer. In fact, when we were in our early twenties we shared an apartment. People would call and ask to speak to "Sarah" and we'd have to ask, "Which one?" There was art school Sarah, and there was under-employed, youth-leader, still-trying-to-figure-out-what-she-could-to-do-with-her-life Sara. No one but my mother called for her.

I'm named after a great-great-grandmother, no one famous at all. Sarah, on the other hand, takes great delight in reminding me that her name is biblical. Which is another way to tell us apart; *she* is the biblical one. I pretty much stick to Jesus while she wants to learn Hebrew so she can study the Psalms in their original language. How are we even friends?

(Digression: There is a modern Yiddish phrase, "*Oy vey*," that expresses dismay or exasperation. Jesus spoke Aramaic so it wasn't in his vernacular, but I can really, really see Jesus saying that. A lot. With a face palm. Especially now.)

When it comes to justice, Sarah is able to articulate her understanding of it. While I get caught up in what's happening around the world, Sarah sees justice as local. She sees it in terms of the individuals in her community.

It reminds me of what South African archbishop Desmond Tutu said: "Do your little bit of good where you are. It's those little bits of good put together that overwhelm the world."

Clearly, I'm a thinker. I can't shut out what is happening in Gaza and Yemen and China. I can't shut out the government policies that created the detention centers at the border with Mexico, or the more recent policies that allow unidentified masked men to snatch people out of their homes or workplaces and off the street. I can't ignore the fact that a third of the prison population in Canada is made up of Indigenous people, and Indigenous women account for almost *half* of the female inmate population in federal prisons. I can't ignore the information that girls as young as nine are circumcised then married to men five times their age. I can't ignore the fact that journalists are deliberately targeted in Gaza so they can't tell the truth about the impact of the war through their words and photos. Too much information, however, stalls out my thinking brain and stops me in my tracks.

Sarah tells me about her father who would go to a local space and help men dealing with addiction. He also doesn't wear anything that isn't a natural fiber like cotton and wool.

How can one small choice make a difference when there is so much injustice to fix, my unfocussed brain wants to know. (Later, when I've had a chance to process this conversation, I realize his choice was a resistance to "fast fashion," a business model that gets trendy clothes to consumers quickly, but has a massive environmental impact.)[37]

My best friend argues that one person doing one thing is meaningful and matters. She told me her church raised tens of thousands of dollars to build a men's shelter in her city and went on to add beds for women. The shelter provides food and shelter for people, plus programs and other supports to help them get back on their feet.

Our conversations about faith usually go like this. I am an ideas person and don't know how to make my ideas a reality. I see too big a picture. In contrast, my friend calmly maintains her one-person-doing-one-thing-helps perspective and slowly brings my big picture into focus and narrows my vision to specific images.

I say we need to address an underlying problem that goes back to society and government, but "jobs and the economy" always seem to be the default reasons why issues like the housing crisis, or accessibility, or addiction, or mental health treatment get pushed aside. Sarah argues patiently for the power of the individual or a group of individuals to address one injustice at a time and to help others on a local level. Her church's successful project proves it's not just an idea.

Our conversation on justice was just one of many conversations we've had over the thirty years of our friendship.

It was exhausting.

It was exhilarating.

It was two people talking about one subject they both feel deeply about but view in two different ways.

So this is what I want to say about the very big, very important, very necessary topic of justice. It's the whole point of the Bible. Even if you aren't into the Bible, you need to know and take heart in the fact that the Bible is very clear about what we are called to do:

> Seek justice.
> Bring forth justice.
> Establish justice.
> Act with justice.
> Do justice.

This is what Jesus grew up hearing at the synagogue. Long before he started his ministry as an adult, he was learning about justice. That's likely why his first public address, the Sermon on the Mount (the Beatitudes), is all about blessing those who think their lives are hard and meaningless and unworthy. Jesus wants us to know that taking care of each other, no matter how small the gesture, is doing justice, because it's the right thing to do. Yet he cautions us by adding, "You follow me, people are going to be skeptical, they're going to push back against what you're saying, they're going to harass you and reject you."[38]

My favorite Frederick Buechner quote is this one: "The place God calls you to is the place where your deep gladness and the world's deep hunger meet."[39]

In other words, what you are passionate about is what the world needs. What matters to you, what inspires and motivates you to take action is what the world is hungry for. That's a great starting point for doing justice. For seeking, bringing forth, establishing, and acting with justice.

Buechner's idea grounds me in the belief that whatever I feel called to do—that feeling that what I am doing is coming from somewhere other than my own shouty, twitchy, doubty mind—the feeling I get when I write a poem or a sermon that simply flows out of me—is the feeling that this work matters more than I realize. That this work is the work of justice.

Pastor and author Emily M. D. Scott wrote, "Wading into preaching about racial injustice means acquainting myself with the suffering of the world and allowing it to do its work on me. My words aren't always graceful and eloquent [but] I figure the best thing I can do is just point to what I see, and hope others see it too. Just uncover the truth we've all been avoiding."[40]

I've also learned that to do justice, the starting point is injustice. We first have to *undo* the injustices. We need to change what is wrong in order to start doing what is right and fair and merciful. We need to find one injustice where we live, in our own community, in our own corner of the world, and fix it.

Fix it, bless it, make it meaningful. Then keep going. Find another injustice to fix. Don't stop. Don't give up, because one person doing one thing—one thing at a time—helps. All those little bits of good add up.

And when the hard work of fixing injustice and doing justice gets too heavy, when the worry and the weary get overwhelming, Jesus invites us to rest with him. We are encouraged to take a break. Rest, breathe, go for a walk near trees, drink a cup of tea. Call a friend.

Because that friend may say exactly what you need to hear in order to keep going to the place where your passion meets someone else's need.

RECKONING

Jesus stands
weeping
at the edge of the abandoned field
stares with unseeing eyes
past the green grass and wildflowers
at what lies beneath

Did they not hear a word I said?
Did they not understand the stories
their meanings
the point of every idea?

Was I too subtle? Too clever?
He wipes his cheeks
How could I have been more specific?

Love one another as I love you
I told them

I could not have stated it any plainer:
Love God
Love each other
Take care of the vulnerable
the weak and the worried
Feed and clothe those who have less
Welcome strangers

Jesus in the World Today

Bring the children to me
I told them
Whoever welcomes a child in my name welcomes me
I told them
Woe to those who harms one of these children
I told them

One
one hundred
one thousand
don't lose count
don't stop counting
don't stop looking

Woe to them
who did this in my name
Woe to the world
who knew and did nothing
Woe to you
who drowns in the truth

Jesus weeps

He falls to his knees
braces his hands against the hard ground
and their voices come to him
as vibrations
through the bleeding wounds in his hands

They are here
They have always been here
They are living still
They are here
They are

my children

RAGING IN THE STREETS

(Inspired by verse 2 of the hymn, "Jesus Christ is Waiting," John L. Bell)

Jesus, peace bringer, peace maker
we don't like to think of you as "raging"
and yet
we have seen what raging in the streets looks like:
cries for peace,
marches for justice,
demands for laws that uphold your law of love.

Perhaps
in our fear of this raging in the streets
our discomfort with protesting and rioting
we forgot to look for you:
to see you in the faces of those in pain because of violence
to see you in the faces of those suffering because of injustice
because of generations of racism and stereotypes and unfairness
to see you in the faces of those struggling under the oppression of
poverty and neglect, ableism and sexism, discrimination and phobias
to see you in the faces of those who stand outside the closed door
those who knock but receive no answer
those who seek but cannot find a friend, a program, a community
those who need to be rescued from abusers
    but whose voices are not heard
those who want to rush in and rescue
    but are held back by policy and police
to see you in the face of the most vulnerable
and the most targeted.

No wonder you are raging in the streets, Jesus
no wonder you are crying out for justice, for peace, for mercy

Jesus in the World Today

for change, for uprising, for your upside-down gospel.

Help us to hear your cries, to respond to your calls
to seek out those who need to find peace and acceptance
to use our abundance and our privilege to do your work
to open up the doors that will shine the light of your love
into the streets
where it belongs

not in the churches
not in the political chambers
not in the courtrooms
not in the corporate headquarters.

Help us to be unafraid
to be brave and bold
in order to be your love in the world
in the streets
where it is needed most.

Amen

9. Turn the Other Cheek

THREE ELEMENTARY SCHOOL STUDENTS got into a fight. All three were suspended even though one of them was defending himself.

This is the dilemma for schools: at home, kids are told by their parents to punch back if someone punches them. When our brain detects a threat and shifts into fight or flight mode, the instinct to fight back can be stronger than the instinct to run away. We might run from a bear or a tiger or someone armed with a knife, but an obnoxious classmate on the soccer field? We instinctively defend ourselves.

But the teachers and principals say if someone punches you or shoves you or says something mean to you, walk away and tell a teacher. Every day at school, we promote the nonviolent response "Hands are not for hitting" and "Feet are not for kicking." (We've had to get more specific because "Keep your hands and feet to yourself" just isn't cutting it anymore.) Every day at school, we promote the idea of turning the other cheek.

That's not what society and culture teaches kids, though, let alone what we teach at home. We tell our kids to be kind, then at the end of the day we release them into a world, possibly into a community, maybe even into a home, that is the opposite of kind and definitely does not turn the other cheek, that wants them to stick up for themselves, to defend themselves.

Our good friend Jesus, however, who seemed possessed of infinite patience and fortitude and the ability to resist slapping someone for being unkind, is the one who said, "If someone slaps your right cheek, turn and give them your left cheek."

He's right, and we know Jesus was all about radical love and radical kindness and changing the system, changing the world, but isn't that a bit much?

Not if you're trying to change the system. Turning the other cheek is next-level kindness. It's also everything Jesus stood for: nonviolent resistance, nonviolent liberation.

Want to overthrow the Romans? Do it without violence.

Want to change the way women are treated? Do it without violence.

Want to change the system that favors the rich and powerful? Do it without violence.

Want mercy and justice for the oppressed? Do it without violence.

Jesus saw—just as we see—how violence only begets more violence, that violence doesn't solve anything and likely makes everything worse, that violence doesn't change the system, doesn't change the way we treat people, doesn't bring about more mercy and justice.

Jesus saw—just as we see—that war does not create peace.

We also see that turning the other cheek does not seem to be the default human reaction. Our amygdala, the part of our brain that processes information and decides how to react, knows fight, flight, freeze, and flop. Turn the other cheek does not compute.

With the call to "turn the other cheek," Jesus references the ancient law regarding "an eye for an eye."[41] This is the idea that an injury should be repaid in kind, and only in kind. It's an attempt to impose fairness and justice by preventing the victim of an injury retaliating by taking his attacker's life, which of course, could create a cycle of feuding and vengeance that lasts for generations.[42]

Jesus takes that to the next level with, "Nope, not even that." His version is, "You have heard that it was said, 'Eye for eye, and tooth for tooth.' But I tell you, if anyone slaps you on the right cheek, turn to them the other cheek also. And if anyone wants your shirt, hand over your coat as well."[43]

You might be thinking, *Seriously? They want my shirt so give them my jacket as well?*

Turn the Other Cheek

According to American theologian and activist Walter Wink, Jesus was pointing to a third way of reacting: not fight, not flight, but an active, nonviolent challenge to the bully, to the oppressor. To find the good news in what Jesus was saying, Wink realized Jesus wasn't advocating for us to let the bully get away with it, to ignore oppression, but to challenge the bully in a completely different way.[44]

We are supposed to take it on the chin and fight back in a nonviolent way. Which sounds about right since we're talking about Jesus. Everything he said has a deeper meaning, a more urgent message. So let's assume Jesus was saying, "Don't react. Don't give someone the satisfaction of responding like they do. Don't lower yourself to their level. Resist violence as a response—always and actively."

Or as Michelle Obama said during the 2016 presidential race, "When they go low, we go high."

That's Jesus talk. Turn the other cheek. Walk away. When they go low, you go high.

No way. That's not right. That's not fair. I can't follow Jesus in this. We need to fight.

Oh, you of little faith. There's more to it. Of course, there is! For Jesus, fight had another meaning. You fought back, but not with violence. We know that a nonviolent response is love and compassion and peace. Kindness. But think bigger. Think relentless versions of all of those. Relentless, constant, committed love, compassion, peace, and kindness. All the time, no matter what.

What? Who on earth could manage to be relentlessly loving and kind all the time? I'm actually starting to sweat here.

Sounds like we need to update our amygdala's operating system with fight, flight, freeze, flop, and … faith. That means peace and love, all the time, in every word thought and spoken, in every action considered and taken, right?

Oof. That's so hard. I think I just fried my amygdala.

The answer, of course, is yes, peace and love, all the time.

Consider what Palestinian Christian pastor and author Rev. Dr. Munther Isaac writes: "My Christian faith requires unwavering commitment to nonviolence, peace, and reconciliation rooted in truth and justice."[45] There's no wiggle room there.

Okay, we know what the problem is so let's stop talking about that and talk about the solution. Not fighting back looks like what? Honestly, I think about this a lot, usually when I'm walking the dog first thing in the morning. What does love in action look like? What does fighting but not fighting mean?

It can be as simple as holding an infant while its parent has a bite to eat at the table next to yours, and as complicated as joining a group of people to sail as close to the shores of Gaza as you can get. It can be as simple as donating food to the after-school food program, and as complicated as sitting in front of a government building with a protest sign.

It means doing what we can to help someone else in the moment, without hesitation, without measuring their worthiness or our own safety. It can be as simple as not indicating to your children that the homeless person hanging around outside the arena is someone to fear. Perhaps instead, indicate that they are worthy of an offering of snacks and water from the vending machine.

One morning, lying in bed after my radio alarm went off just before the five o'clock news, I caught the tail end of an interview that sounded very interesting. I jotted down a name so I could search out the interview later and learn more. Father John Dear is a long-time peace activist and the author of many books and articles about peace and nonviolence. Dear breaks down living a life of nonviolence into three practices that we all must do. All three, not just one.

1. You have to be totally nonviolent toward yourself.
2. You have to be meticulously nonviolent toward every human being in your life, every human being you'll ever meet, every human being on the planet, and all the creatures, as well as the planet itself.
3. You have to have one foot in the global grassroots movement of nonviolence, as a proponent for justice, disarmament, and

the environment. Once you step into one of those issues, you realize they're all connected.

Father Dear says people tell him it's impossible but that they're really good at one of those things. To this he responds, "That's the problem. There are billions of people who are really peaceful and nice. That is not gospel nonviolence."[46]

Now there's the rub: *gospel* nonviolence. The way Jesus did it. The way he showed us to do it. To do everything differently. To be whole-life committed to his way of love and peace, to nonviolent resistance and liberation, to taking care of each other. Listening and welcoming and feeding and blessing. But for some reason we just can't get on board fully with what he asked of us. We can't let go of the need to feel some kind of control over our lives, and the stuff we worked so hard to accumulate. We can't let go of the thirst for violence, the hunger for greed, the appetite for power. The need to judge and shame others, to exclude others, to oppress and hurt and even kill others.

The truth is being kind isn't just being nice to each other. It isn't just smiles and hugs and compliments. It isn't just taking food to someone in crisis; it isn't just making a donation to an animal shelter or donating wool socks to an outreach center.

We are called to do kindness the way Jesus did. Exactly like he did. Radically and relentlessly. With nonviolence. Not just by speaking words of love and peace but by *doing* the work of love and peace. All. The. Time.

Does Father John Dear think it's possible? Does he think people can really do this work?

After all this time? After all this time not doing it? He says, "It's the struggle of ordinary people to keep at it. We have to live our lives, but we have to be detached from the outcome, the results."[47]

Meaning, keep at it. Keep trying. At home, at school, in the community, at your job. Don't think about if it's working, just do it. Just as Jesus did it. He didn't worry about the outcome—about his death or what would happen after he died. He didn't think about his legacy. And look at the outcome: We have our faith because he lived his life.

THE PROTEST

It was hot
hotter than ever
hotter than it should be

the crowd was large
larger than ever
larger than anyone thought it could be

and the crowd was diverse
more diverse than it ever had been
all ages
all sizes
all colours
every single person
who cared
who worried
who was scared
who had a voice
and a sign
a kid
a grandparent
a friend
had showed up
to be seen and heard
to be counted
to be part of
what would be
what needed to be
a new earth
a new creation

The Protest

Oh, the signs!
There is no Planet B
Respect your mother
Planet over profit
Earth is our home

Jesus looked around
and heard the chants
heard the singing
saw the signs

the signs of a revolution
the signs of a new and improved covenant
love God
love your neighbours
love the earth

and he held his sign up a little higher
OUR PLANET IS
HOLY GROUND

he wondered if anyone would notice
the small print
what he had written around the edges

Blessed are you who
feed the hungry
fill the glass of those thirsting for justice
welcome refugees
provide for those who can't afford
food clothing shelter medicine
care for the sick
abolish prisons

he'd tried to change the system
once before
and again and again

Jesus in the World Today

the scars in his palms throbbed
as he remembered the power of a crowd
that chants
that demands
that follows the leader
that has to see to believe

the power of a system
to triumph over insistent demands for change
simply by ignoring
all the signs

10. Love the Earth

WE DON'T USUALLY ASSOCIATE Jesus with "care for creation," do we? ("Care for creation" is the phrase that always comes up as a focus in conversations about the earth and the environment.) Jesus is the guy who talked a lot about the poor and the vulnerable; about how we should turn the other cheek, give the guy who stole our shirt our coat as well. He's the one who talked about love, a lot.

You better believe, however, that Jesus in the world today would care for creation. How does Jesus fit into the climate crisis? As part of his radical ministry of love, Jesus condensed the Mosaic laws from ten to two: Love God and love your neighbor. Perhaps for the too-hot-to-handle twenty-first century, Jesus would make his commandment three-fold: Love God, love your neighbor, and love the earth.

The thing about Jesus' commandment is that it applies to everyone—neighbor, stranger, alien (a nod to our current deep space exploration), and even to those who make us uncomfortable, those whose behavior contradicts the Ten Commandments, let alone Jesus' commands, actions we aren't prepared to do because they're hard or involve giving something up, or might get us arrested.

Wait. Jesus is one of those people who makes us uncomfortable, isn't he, because by loving each other, Jesus meant these six things:

> feed the hungry,
> give drink to the thirsty,
> welcome foreigners,
> clothe the naked,
> care for the sick,
> visit those in prison.[48]

When we take these verses literally, read them shallowly, when we don't really think about what they mean, we miss the vastness, the expansiveness, the not-as-obvious-but-now-makes-total-sense-ness of Jesus' statement.

Jesus advocated for the kind of hospitality that offers a helping hand to people, to plants and creatures of all kinds regardless of what risk there might be; the kind of hospitality that puts the needs of others before our own needs, that treats others the way we want to be treated—with respect and dignity, compassion and mercy. This applies not just to other people, but to cows and goats, to migratory birds and fish in the sea, to worms and bees. Especially to bees.

Visiting those in prison? Perhaps we are called to bail out those jailed for protesting pipelines. Maybe it's not even a literal prison but an overcrowded refugee camp or detention center. Perhaps we are called to abolish prisons altogether, especially considering they are disproportionately filled with people who are Black and Indigenous.

Could "clothe the naked" also apply to affordable housing? To making sure everyone has adequate shelter that is safe and secure? To allowing house-less citizens to make camp in public spaces, rather than calling in police to remove them?

Why *wouldn't* Jesus' six calls to action apply to climate change as well? Can we honestly claim to know Jesus and believe he'd sit this one out?

Nope. There goes Jesus, in the middle of the marching crowd, holding up a sign that reads,

SYSTEM CHANGE
NOT CLIMATE CHANGE

Jesus is all about changing the system. Whether it was 30 CE or today in almost 2030 CE.

And who was he changing the system *for*? The meek. The hungry and the thirsty. The merciful, the pure in heart, the peacemakers. The persecuted and the reviled. Especially the poor.

Climate change and natural disasters—like heat waves and droughts, wildfires and flooding, hurricanes and tornadoes—have a far greater impact on those living in poverty. According to Mercy Corps, an international non-governmental humanitarian agency, in 2019 nearly 400 events affected 95 million people globally and caused $103 billion in economic losses.[49]

The damages caused by these events are nearly impossible for families living in poverty to overcome. Droughts alone impact around 55 million people every year and the damage hits the agriculture industry—the primary source of food and income for many people in developing countries—particularly hard.

One day in July 2022, CNN actually led its top-of-the-hour newscast by reporting on the heat wave in Europe. The network led with a story about climate change! The reporter in Italy detailed the impact on crops, particularly rice fields, that the devastating heat wave was having. In fact, a rice farmer said the impact of climate change had been affecting his rice fields for a decade.

Clearly, it's not just the Third World that feels the devastating impact of climate change. Already, those who can afford home and property insurance are finding their coverage more expensive and less inclusive as natural disasters sweep through communities. The more devastating impacts of climate change include the loss of homes and property, and in some cases livelihoods, as well as the unbearable tragedy of the loss of life.

As I edited this book in the summer of 2025, on the east coast of Canada, we reached extreme drought conditions by mid-September, with no significant rainfall since June. This drought has impacted our farmers and the produce we count on them to harvest and sell. The soil is dry, and so is the grass, and so are the woods. We are all anxious about wildfires.

Mercy Corps says three out of four people living in poverty rely on agriculture and natural resources to survive. When agriculture and natural resources are damaged and even destroyed by natural disasters, those who live in poverty find it much harder to survive.

Okay, so what Jesus says applies to climate change. But does he give any suggestions about what to do, how to act, what to say? Of course he does. This is Jesus, after all: "If you don't give up everything you have, you can't be my disciple."[50]

Let's consider this statement in the context of the climate crisis. To become followers of Jesus, we must give up our stuff. Give up everything that runs on a fossil fuel. Give up the coffee cups and the takeout containers. Give up the new smart phone. Give up the coffee pods. Give up the plastic bags and the plastic water bottles.

(My long-time thinking has been to give up air-conditioning as well, or at least use it sparingly and not frigidly, but air conditioning may now be a justice issue. Age and health conditions are some of the reasons why people must have air conditioning. As my editor pointed out, "Not everyone can tough it out," and people living on the streets need cooling centers that use air conditioning, too. Dogs and cats suffer in extreme heat, as well.)

Are we willing and able to follow Jesus by giving up all our stuff?

While riding in a boat during a storm, Jesus asks his fearful companions, "Do you still have no faith?"[51] In the context of Creation and our impact on it, we can interpret this as Jesus reminding us that we created this planetary mess. The storm we are caught in is of our own making.

Our sleep—our comfort—will be disturbed by the chaos and catastrophe we have failed to prevent.

Where has our faith been all these years? If we call ourselves Christians; if we are disciples of Jesus; if we follow his way, his truth, and his life, where was our faith? Jesus called us to do six specific things. Just six! And all of them are things we'd want done for us if our life, our world, suddenly and unexpectedly went sideways.

Love the Earth

When we think of creation, we think of the first chapters of Genesis, the origin stories of the world and of people. For the ancients, the Genesis story was in part about God's relationship with creation. For Christians, the good news is about God's relationship with humanity. It's about love and friendship. It's about ethics. It's about doing what is best for each other in community. It's about taking care of each other, and that means taking care of our planet and its life-sustaining resources.

This is where we find ourselves as Jesus followers during the human-created climate crisis. Since we are people of hope, we are called to be part of the good news and the good work of caring for creation, because we are called to love God, love each other, and love the earth.

JESUS, TAKE THE WHEEL

Jesus, take the wheel
as we drive down this highway
bumper to bumper trying to escape
the flames rushing towards the city
the smoke billowing through our streets
the air choked with particles
with pain fear grief

Jesus, take the wheel
as we drive through this water
stalling out in the depths we didn't see coming
swept away by the currents of our own failure
to act to respond to prepare

Jesus, take the wheel
as we drive through this hail
this swirling wind
this debris flinging itself around
in quiet neighborhoods filled with people
just trying to make ends meet
make it to the end of the month
make a better life for themselves

Jesus, take the wheel
take over
as we take cover
take apart
what we have wrought
through our selfishness
arrogance
ignorance
refusal to believe

Jesus, Take the Wheel

Jesus, take the wheel
and put into park
all the polluting of our minds
with fake news and flawed "facts"
conspiracy theories and claims of collusion
turn off the engines of
our obsession with stuff
cheap and plastic
our resistance to driving less
our reluctance to growing more
unhitch our reliance to fuels
that harm more than they help
keep us warm keep us cool

Jesus, take the wheel
and take us to a new era
of everything in moderation
of carpooling and car sharing
of transit and trains
take us back to the moment
you know so well
when everyone hears the message
and wants to follow
but when the time comes to actually
change
do things differently
sacrifice
we kill the messenger

take us back
and hand us the wheel
give us the chance to take a different path
follow a different route
make better choices
than the ones that got us here
burning

boiling
drowning
crying out
forsaken

HEAVEN ON EARTH

Jesus,
the stories tell us how you
healed with a touch
calmed storms with a look
fed crowds with a wave of your hands

you walked on water
you slept in the middle of a storm

you made it look so easy

you showed us how to be kind and merciful
how to be just and fair,
how loving those who have less and need more
how giving more and taking less
how planting the smallest seed of hope
can grow an entire field of peace
how these are the keys to the kingdom
here on earth

Earth is the kin-dom
heaven on earth
where we live is the kin-dom
the community of heaven
here on earth

you made it look so easy

Jesus in the World Today

and here we are
rushing downstream
caught in a current
clinging to trees

washed away
washed out
washed up on the shore
where you stood unrecognized

and here we are
hoping for the best
even as we refuse to prepare for the worst
refuse to acknowledge the worst is yet to come

if only fools rush in
who is saving us
who is searching and rescuing
who is recovering
who is suffering the fools

we are so proud of ourselves
how we help how we support others
how we come together in a crisis

yet we refuse to see we are the architects of the crisis
we create the heat dome
we create the atmospheric river
we create the seismic anomaly
the hurricane the tornado the wildfire the flood
the coastal erosion the mud slides
we are wind and fire and water and earth

Jesus,
your stories tell us how we can
heal with our hands

Heaven on Earth

calm storms feed crowds
walk on water
if we believe we can

we are the saviors
we are the fools

and here we are building our houses on the sand
at the edge
the edge of tomorrow
we won't worry about tomorrow
we won't worry about
what we'll eat what we'll wear where we'll live
until we realize the storms are here today

and here we are
breathing underwater
breathing fire
holding our breath
can't catch our breath

can't catch a break

heartbroken
broken down
broken open

by destruction
by death
by loss and longing
not again
if only
what if
why us
why now

Jesus in the World Today

we believe in climate change
we believe in the weather we have wrought
we believe we are the key to saving the kingdom

yet we resist calls to save ourselves

help our unbelief

11. Plant What Will Grow

I LOVE BEE BALM. I love its colors, red and deep fuchsia and light lavender. I love its spiky flowers and strong, peppery scent. I love its name—*bee balm*. Balm. Something soothing for the bees in a world that is dropping pesticide bombs on them.

For all the love I have for bee balm, however, I cannot get it to survive on my property. I probably spent $100 over a couple of summers just on bee balm plants, and so far not one returned the following spring.

I love clematis. I love its colors, whether a deep purple or a light pink. I love its wide-open flowers. I love the feathery seed puffs left after the leaves fall off. I love its name—*clematis*. It means ingenuity and cleverness because of its climbing prowess. I have several thriving clematis plants. They love growing on my property. So I bought another one.

I plant what will grow.

I saw that phrase—plant what will grow—somewhere and wrote it down on a piece of paper because I knew it was the perfect line for a sermon when everything is lush and green and growing. You also need to know that I bought another bee balm, and planted it in a new spot, a tried-and-true spot of good soil and lots of sunshine. Why? Why would I plant something that will not grow beyond one season?

Hope. That's why.

If the clematis represents love and joy, bee balm represents hope and persistence. It represents the hope that if I try something different, if I don't give up, if I'm down on my knees in the dirt saying a persistent prayer over this new plant, this time it will grow.

However, this is the last time, the very last time, I'm planting bee balm. I promise. While I don't want to give up until I've exhausted all attempts, the spot it's in right now is my final option. If it can't grow in that spot, with the sunshine and good soil, if it doesn't come back next spring, there will be no bee balm in my gardens.

You're probably thinking, *Give it up already!* Just plant what will grow! And you're likely right.

But what if the early Jesus followers had given up? What if those apostles and new followers had given in to the pressures of the religious leaders and their familiar, long-established laws? What if, instead of steadfastly nurturing the seeds Jesus had planted, instead of protecting the seedlings, instead of being persistent about their prayers, what if they'd given up, turned their backs on Jesus' teachings, claimed they were too hard to understand, spreading the good news too much work? What if they'd given up on his hope for the future and the all-inclusive resort of God and instead put their faith in the kingdoms of, well, kings (and CEOs and presidents)?

There is an argument for thinking that in many ways we—collectively as Christians—have given up on Jesus' teachings; that, in many ways, we aren't nurturing and protecting those seeds Jesus planted and that we haven't tended the vision of the world he gave us.

We can do better. We need to do better. Collectively. As Christians, as Jesus followers, as people of faith, and as human beings.

Even if it just means changing our attitude about one thing, like being careful about what our children and grandchildren hear us say about other people. Because every word that comes out of our mouths is a *seed*. It gets planted in the heart and mind of someone else and it grows there.

It grows into a prickly, thistly bush that only hurts those who try to care for it, or it grows into a tall and joyful sunflower that inspires compassion and mercy for others.

Plant What Will Grow

We know what we are supposed to do because Jesus showed us, and he told us. Even if others say it shouldn't be done, that there are rules and laws to follow, we are called to do what Jesus would do.

"Stretch out your hand," Jesus said, and he healed the withered hand. On the Sabbath.[52]

Stretch out your hand. An easy command. A simple gesture. A profound, life-altering action.

Like adding water and sunlight to a dry, withering plant. A bit of water, a bit of light, and everything is better. Everything is better when we love each other. When we care for each other. When we treat each other with even a little bit of kindness.

That's what the early Jesus followers—the first Christians—had: just enough water, just enough light, just enough love to keep them going, to keep their faith and their hope alive.

That seems to be what we get these days in the twenty-first century. For every moment of terror and horror, we get an act of kindness, a measure of mercy. We see the hand reaching out, the hand offering healing.

Thank God for those moments.

I honestly don't think we could keep going if we didn't have the action—pain and suffering—followed by an equal and opposite reaction—love and comfort.

So plant what will grow. Protect the seeds, nurture them, watch over them.

Persist. Pray. Don't give up.

But it's also like my bee balm and clematis. Why keep trying with one plant when another does so well? When a whole bunch of others—phlox and columbine and hollyhocks and rudbeckia—do so well? Let others who do bee balm well do the bee balm.

In your faithful, spirit-led living, focus on what works well, focus on what you are good at nurturing. We aren't called to keep working at a lost cause once our attempts to help and heal are exhausted. We are called to use our talents to their best use—to grow tomatoes, write poems, knit prayer shawls, build bookshelves and rocking chairs, play music, bake cookies, sew quilts, say the right thing at the right time, and smile at everyone. In other words, to plant seeds that will grow, remembering also that "No seed ever sees the flower."

That's a Zen proverb but it describes Jesus, doesn't it? He was the seed. He planted the new way, the new truth, the new life, but he never saw it flower. He didn't witness the creation of an entire faith built, for the most part, on his two commandments to love God and each other.

Two small seeds with the potential to grow into great big self-propagating plants with deep, deep roots.

We are in charge of those seeds. We are in charge of bringing to flower what Jesus planted and continues to plant in each of us.

By using the seeds of persistence, selflessness, compassion, and a passion for justice planted in us, we continue to nurture the life and ministry of Jesus; we continue to water and fertilize the garden of love Jesus planted, through droughts and winds, through hot sunshine and heavy rains, in spite of the bugs eating and squirrels digging, chickens scratching and dogs burying bones in the gardens ...

We continue to water and fertilize those seeds no matter what the world throws at us.

We continue to stretch out our hand and believe anything is possible.

PLANTING SEEDS

"Hey, are you the gardener?"

Jesus straightens
steps his foot off the blade of his shovel
smacks the loose soil from his gloves
and turns around

"You say that I am,"
Jesus replies

"Well, we've been following the path
and we can't figure out what kind of garden this is."

Gloved hands gripping the handle,
Jesus leans into his shovel

"What do you think it is?"
Jesus asks

"Well, some areas are rocky
and nothing much is growing there.
Then there's an area all grown up in thistles,
which are very prickly, let me tell you.
We tried pulling out a few
because they were choking off some plants.
Look at our hands!"

Jesus doesn't take off his gloves
and show them his hands

Jesus in the World Today

"And now this area,
where all this soil is turned over
like it's ready for planting.
It looks like good ground,
like stuff will really grow in it."

Jesus shifts his weight to his other foot
digging always bothers that scar in his side

"But look at those weeds at the edges!
Don't you know they will mix in with everything else
and ruin the garden?"

Jesus looks at the dandelions
growing in the grassy area at his feet
he watches a bumblebee
fly from one flower to the next,
buzzing loudly
as it collects bright yellow pollen
this is his favorite miracle
how a big fuzzy body with such small wings
manages to fly
like the bee simply believes it can

"Why is nothing growing in this garden?
There is all this space, all this potential,
but nothing is growing.
Why don't you get rid of the rocks and thistles?
Why don't you fill up the empty spaces?
We just can't figure out what kind of garden this is."

"You have eyes to see and ears to hear,"
Jesus says

He takes a seed packet out of his pocket
hands it over

Planting Seeds

"These seeds are so small!
And it will take so long for them to grow.
Don't you have plants ready to go in the ground?"

"The ones that are ready don't need me,"
Jesus says

"What? What kind of gardener are you?
Here, take your seeds. Plant them yourself.
We're going to find a proper garden,
where the flowers and trees are already growing.
That's where we belong.
Not here among the rocks and the thistles and the empty soil."

"What is hidden will grow,"
Jesus says
"What you don't see now will become the life you seek."

but they are too far away to hear him

CALLING IN THE STREETS

(Inspired by verse 5 of the hymn, "Jesus Christ is Waiting," John L. Bell)

Jesus,
you call to us –
from the streets,
from the rooftops,
from the corners and edges,
from the shadows.
You call to us—
to join your journey,
to walk away from everything we think we know,
to walk with you and follow your way.

Forgive us for all the times
we don't stop to listen to what you are saying,
we brush past you as if you are
a street corner prophet shouting about the end of days.

Forgive us for the all the times
we ignore your call
especially the one we hear in our hearts
in those moments when we are relaxed or half-asleep,
doing something that allows our mind to still
and the truth of our spirit to speak clearly.

Forgive us for refusing to listen to your voice,
forgive us for ignoring your call to sharing and showing and doing,
forgive us for allowing our fears
of change,
of different,
of others
to drown out your call for justice, mercy and humility.

Calling in the Streets

Call to us now, Jesus,
catch us unawares as we stop and wonder
whose voice that is
calling to us from the streets,
from the school, from the detention center,
from the mountain top, from the garden,
from the wilderness,
calling us to follow and believe and become.

Amen

12. Where Is Your Treasure?

THERE WAS A MOMENT about a month into the pandemic lockdown of 2020 that I sensed we were on the cusp of something grand.

People around the world were staying home, off the streets, away from work; they were singing from their balconies and rallying behind health-care providers who were working long hours and extra shifts. People realized how much we need those who pour our coffee, stock grocery store shelves, deliver goods. They checked in on neighbors and dropping off food on doorsteps—often without being asked to. It felt like we were on the cusp of realizing our potential.

It felt like we were *thisclose* to stepping onto a new path, a path we know as the Way of Love; a path of compassion and peace, justice and mercy, hospitality and acceptance, of taking care of each other.

We were *thisclose* to understanding what the phrase "the common good" means.

"The common good" refers to what is beneficial to as many people as possible in a community. It's what we, collectively, can achieve as one human society. It's the idea that we all have certain interests in common and thus we have an obligation to make sure everyone gets a fair share.

The principle of "the common good" has never been widely put into practice because so many of us balk at the idea of sharing our abundance. We don't know what fair looks like. We worry we will end up with less if others get more. Jobs and the economy and payouts to shareholders are deemed more important than social programs that support our most vulnerable and those we need to take care of.

The "common good" reminds us that we're all in this together so we must take care of each other. Even if it means we have to give up something to make life better for others, we do it because it is morally right. We do it because it's what Jesus wants us to do. If you need my sweater, I'll give you my shirt, too. Because I probably have four more at home.

Remember what happened at the start of the pandemic? We panic-purchased toilet paper. We stocked up to the point of hoarding it. When you hoard anything—money, food, water, or toilet paper—you end up with more than you need, perhaps even more than you'll ever use. This means others likely go without. That's definitely not fair.

Risk experts explain that we bought toilet paper in such quantities because 1. It was cheap; and 2. It made us feel like we were doing something.[53] Buying and hoarding toilet paper gave us a sense of control at a time when we couldn't control what was happening. It was an emotional response, and one of the strongest human emotions is fear (another is anger). So much of what we say and do that is harmful and selfish is done when we are fearful.

Human biology is wired for survival, for fight or flight, for strength over weakness. It's why we need constant reminders to treat others the way we want to be treated, and to love each other. Love during a pandemic means, among many other things, making sure there's enough toilet paper to go around.

Thankfully, as often happens, a hopeful side to this pandemic story emerged. The opposite of pandemic hoarding was pandemic care packages. Rather than hoarding food, people shared it. They cooked and baked, then shared it with neighbors. They went grocery shopping and bought extra. They looked out for those who couldn't leave their homes, or those without the means to have extras in their life at a time when they were isolated.

In any situation, even the worst, we are faced with the choice—to hoard or to help. To share what we have or keep to it to ourselves.

What are we called to do?

Jesus says, "Don't worry about what you have or don't have. You will always have what you need."[54]

We are supposed to have faith that our basic needs will be met; that we will have food and clothes and shelter; that maybe we'll live in a really nice shelter with no neighbors living too close by; and that we'll have more than one pair of shoes and put on weight because our freezers are so well stocked …

Wait a minute! We get what we need—and then we want more.

That's what happens. That's how we see abundance. Not in terms of having *enough*, but in terms of having *more*. And, for some people, it's about having more than anybody else.

We tend to get a little clingy with our money and our stuff; we are afraid of losing it all.

Yet Jesus says, "Don't worry. You will always have what you need."

Jesus hasn't met many people, has he? He hasn't met politicians or CEOs or property developers. Oh, wait, of course he has. They're the reason he's still relevant today—because some people don't get their basic needs fulfilled while others take more than they need. Some people hoard resources while others go without.

How many of us wore the same two or three outfits over the weeks and months of the lockdown? Despite closets and drawers full of clothes?

When you think about what's in your home, what you own and use, what's on your shelves and in your drawers, how much of it was purchased to fulfill a "want," rather than a true "need"? Most of us have what we need, and then some. When we have more than we need, we are called to share that abundance.

In an article about the "economy of abundance" in *Emergence Magazine*, Potawatomi author Robin Wall Kimmerer wrote, "In a gift economy, wealth is understood as having enough to share, and the practice of dealing with abundance is to give it away." In the same article, she mused, "What if scarcity is just a cultural construct?"[55]

What if? After all, according to Jesus, we will always have what we need. And of course, we already have more than we need.

In the end, what is true abundance anyway? It's really everything we can't buy.

We are so busy worrying about *having* enough and *being* enough, about what's gone wrong and what could go wrong, that we often forget to acknowledge the abundance already present in our lives, already sustaining us.

We acknowledge our abundance when we realize we have enough blessings of peace, love, mercy, grace, and kindness to share with others, to be in service to others. To our neighbors *here* and around the *world*.

If your basic needs are met—if you have enough food, a warm coat, a bed, and a roof over your head—what *really* makes your life worth living and brings meaning and purpose to your life? A satisfying job. Friends. Family, if you're lucky. A pet to love and care for, if you're so inclined. Joy. Laughter. Hope. Peace. Safety. Connection.

As Jesus said, "For where your treasure is, there will your heart be also."[56]

JESUS' BIRTHDAY

"Hey, Jesus,
I hear you have a birthday coming up,"
Philip says
as they sit around the table on the patio
in the evening shade of a pomegranate tree

Jesus preached at the local church
that afternoon
and now he and his friends
are having supper
at a small restaurant on the edge of town
where they are the only customers

Jesus always chooses the places
that look like they'll appreciate
the arrival of a dozen or so diners

"Judas told us it's your thirtieth," Philip adds
"Of course he did," Jesus replies
nodding at his long-time friend

He takes a sip of wine
he doesn't want his birthday acknowledged
let alone celebrated
doesn't want a party or gifts
not even a nice chocolate cake
just for him
most people don't even know
what his birth date is
but leave it to Judas
to betray his confidence

Jesus' Birthday

"30!" Thomas shouts
the one with all the enthusiasm
"Dude, that deserves a party!"

"You know Jesus won't have a party
just for himself," Judas smirks
"We need to make it a party for everyone!
That works with your philosophy, doesn't?
Inviting everyone to the party?"

Peter flips open his laptop
"Let's check the schedule
and see what we can plan."
In a few key strokes
he opens their travel itinerary and
schedule of speaking engagements

Jesus prefers to wander from place to place
letting the spirit lead him to where he needs to be
but his friends insist on setting up events
and announcing his arrival
they want a big audience
they want important people to show up
and as many social media influencers as possible

Jesus likes to keep a low profile
because so often
he causes a bit of a stir
once he gets going
his passion for justice and mercy
often gets the best of him
he hasn't flipped any tables yet
but sometimes he feels the urge
just to make a point

Jesus in the World Today

"There isn't a break until we reach
Bethlehem," says Peter

Jesus watches a small, brown bird
flit through the branches of the pomegranate tree
he's always reminding them
to block out periods of time
for prayer
but Judas complains
everyone just lies around and naps
when Jesus goes off on his own

"That just happens to be
where Jesus was born," Judas says

"That's perfect!
Celebrating Jesus' thirtieth birthday
in the place he was born!"

"So many people will show up for that.
This will be the event of the year!"

"There's that new hotel that's just opened up.
I bet if we hold the party there
they'll comp us rooms
maybe even the food."

"There has to be a DJ in Bethlehem
who'll do the music in exchange for exposure."

Jesus watches the sun drop behind the low hills
sure, he wants to engage with an audience
but he doesn't want to influence the affluent
he wants to transform the lives of
the poor the meek the mourning
the neglected the ignored the persecuted

Jesus' Birthday

he wants women considered equals
and everyone to get a fair chance
no matter who no matter what

He wonders
why his birthday is such a big deal
why there will be gifts
and too much food
and people who have to work
while everyone else is partying

he knows he'll end up in the kitchen
washing dishes
meeting people and hearing stories
he won't forget
instead of networking
in the crowd of strangers
who don't even know
whose birthday it is

and he wonders
why his birthday matters to anyone
except his mother
who always claims
an angel appeared
at the foot of her hospital bed
on the night he was born

DANCING IN THE STREETS

(Inspired by verse 4 of the hymn, "Jesus Christ is Waiting," John L. Bell)

Oh, boogie-woogie Jesus,
if only defeating hatred and bigotry
was as easy as dancing!
Then we'd all be dancing fools, wouldn't we?
Twirling and tapping, jiving and jumping for you
in the streets, showing everyone what love looks like
Right?
We would,
wouldn't we?

We ask for forgiveness, Jesus, for every moment
when we were asked to dance with compassion
but shook our head no;
when we were asked to dance with justice
but refused to take the hand held out to us;
when we were asked to dance with peace
but we turned away and turned up the music
till it was too loud to hear.

We pray for courage, Jesus, for every moment
when we are asked to dance
to your tune,
to hear your music inside us
and respond,
to let go of our inhibitions
and follow your lead across the floor, and into the streets.

Dancing in the Streets

Make us dancing fools, DJ JC, so that the whole world sees
what love looks like:
acceptance and humility
mercy and healing
with arms open wide and a seat at the table
when we need to rest our legs.

Make us dancing fools so that whole world hears
what your music sounds like:
joy and equality
laughter and welcome
with everybody on the dance floor,
everybody joining in the street party.

Where there is no fear, no distrust, no profiling
where all your people
are dancing in the streets,
in your name,
in the name of love.

Amen

13. It Doesn't Add Up

THE ORIGINS OF LABOR Day, the first Monday in September, lie in the labor union movement of the late 1880s, which included the eight-hour-day movement, which advocated for eight hours for work, eight hours for recreation, and eight hours for rest.

Jesus said, "Come to me, those of you who labor and are heavy laden, and I will give you rest"[57] or as other versions put it, "Come to me, those of you who are weary and burdened, and I will give you rest." No matter the words used, the point is the same: Jesus offers rest.

Rest from our work, rest from our burdens, rest from our worries, and even from the never-ending fight for justice, fairness, equality, inclusion, and dignity. Not to mention affordable housing and universal healthcare.

Jesus understood that in order to love our neighbors as ourselves, to keep taking care of each other no matter how hard it gets, we need to rest, to take breaks, to take care of ourselves.

It never ceases to amaze me how Jesus and his ideas, his calls to action, remain utterly relevant for our time. Whether we're talking about rest, or the poor.

You know, the poor who are always with us.[58]

Which is why I want to talk about math.

I have no idea if Jesus was good at math (although he did multiply the loaves and fishes), but it turns out our attitudes towards math and how we teach it have created a great inequality similar to the inequality created by our attitudes toward poverty.

It Doesn't Add Up

A lot of us claim we're not good at math, we can't do math, we hate math. That's why many children believe the same thing. They hear it at home and they hear it from some teachers, too. They hear that girls can't do math; they hear that they aren't born with the ability to do math. By age six, many students already show signs of math anxiety.[59] Truth is, our struggles with math have nothing to do with gender. Or genetics.

Canadian author and mathematician John Mighton says everyone can do math because it's not a gift of ability that only a few of us are born with.[60] He claims that the way we teach math and the pervasive negative attitude towards math contribute to our failure to help children learn math and actually like math. Thus, we are wasting our potential.

For the record, this guy isn't just a single-minded, brilliant mathematician; he's also an award-winning playwright, so he's good both at math and with words.

Here's how this relates to labor. In his latest book, Mighton shares a story about students enrolled in a nursing program who were unable to pass the first-year math course required to continue in the program. Noting this repeating pattern, the course instructor did a "math boot camp" a week before school started using Mighton's teaching methods. Her students passed the first-year math course with an average B grade.[61]

Talk about wasted potential. How many nurses did we lose out on because many students had a deeply ingrained idea that they weren't good at math? It's kind of like believing that only one person (Jesus) can change the world, can love his neighbor and his enemy, can help the poor.

Just as we all have the potential and the ability to learn to do math, we all have the potential and the ability to help the poor. *All of us.* We are reminded of this by the words of Jesus, "You always have the poor with you."[62] It's usually quoted out of context and those eight words are often twisted to mean, *Oh, okay, if the poor will always be around—shrug, shrug—I can ignore the issue and not do anything to assist those living in poverty.* This is Jesus, though, and in the words of the late Pope Francis, "In everything, Jesus teaches that poverty is not the result of fate, but a concrete sign pointing to his presence among us. We do not find him when and where we want, but see him in the lives of the poor, in their sufferings and needs, in the often-inhuman conditions in which they are forced to live."[63]

Jesus would be delighted, I'm sure, that a growing number of people are advocating for a Basic Guaranteed Income or Basic Income Guarantee or Universal Basic Income. What it's called depends on your state or province or your church denomination: for example, The United Church of Canada calls it "Guaranteed Livable Income."[64] A basic guaranteed income would be a regular, unconditional payment sent by the government to individuals that would be enough to ensure they can meet their basic needs and live with dignity, regardless of their work status.[65]

The 2020 pandemic really highlighted how many families and individuals live at or below the poverty line. To be honest, I haven't paid much attention to the idea, or to the lack of movement on the issue because—shrug, shrug—what does it have to do with me? What do the poor have to do with me?

Ah, Jesus, how you love to show me the answer. Two things happened that opened my eyes and made me see differently.

The first was an online article about a one-year pilot project in Denver, Colorado, in the year 2022 that claims that a basic guaranteed income made a huge difference in the lives of the people who received it, which included those who were homeless and living in shelters or cars or in tents.

I don't know why I clicked on the article, but what caught my attention was the clearly stated "debunking" of the common objections to the program. One of the reasons touted for *not* creating a basic guaranteed income is that we can't afford it because we're paying for things like policing and social services and health care. But the pilot project in Denver found that those costs actually *decreased*, because the city didn't spend as much money on things like shelters and emergency calls.[66]

The program works. It makes a difference. The city of Denver decided to continue with the basic guaranteed income program—*because it works*. However, the program was cancelled in 2025 by the mayor.[67]

The second thing happened in my Master of Education program. The first course educators take is about equity and social justice, and on the final day of the course, our instructor talked about the Basic Income Guarantee. What I learned shocked me. In Canada, we've known for fifty years that it works. Fifty years. We still haven't implemented it, though, because of the widespread belief that it's a handout and will be misused. This resistance is an insurmountable obstacle.

Canada's first experiment with a Basic Annual Income, as it was called, happened in Manitoba between 1974 and 1979. According to an article published in *Broadview* magazine in March 2024, "The impacts were swift and dramatic. People got their cavities filled. Families were able to afford fresh fruit and vegetables. Teenagers went back to school and received their diplomas."[68]

That's a hallelujah, right? Now we have fifty years of facts and research and evidence to back the claim that a basic annual income works and reduces the costs of other social services, yet we have not implemented it.

One letter to the editor in response to that article in *Broadview* magazine repeated the same old trope about people using the money to buy booze and smokes and lottery tickets and a larger television. Another letter writer concluded with these words, "Sorry to say it, but poverty has always been with us and always will be."[69]

And that's a problem. We misuse or misunderstand Jesus' statement, "You will always have the poor among you." We twist those words to let us off the hook. We'll never be rid of the poor and they're just going to waste the money, so why bother?

Jesus challenged the hypocrisy of the disciples, who were probably more interested in criticizing the woman who poured the oil than in actually helping the poor. In essence, Jesus was *really* saying, if you're so concerned about the poor, what are *you* going to do about it. What Jesus is *really* saying to us in the twenty-first century is, not only is poverty not going away, it's worse, so what are you doing about it?

Which brings me back to math. The belief that math is only for a few smart people, that boys do math better than girls, that if you don't get math immediately you'll *never* get math, are simply misinformed, misguided beliefs. They are not founded in facts or research or evidence.

The same is true of our beliefs about poverty; they are misinformed and misguided and aren't founded in facts or research or evidence. We have a deeply ingrained prejudice against people who live in poverty. We assume it's their fault; we assume they are milking the benefits system.

One of the teachers in my MEd class said that, where she lives and works, a lot of families are one injury away from poverty. One injury away from poverty. Imagine the stress of living like that. Many of you may have witnessed or experienced the insecurity and anxiety that comes with losing an income.

When I told a friend I was going to talk about this at church, she immediately shared her example of the failure of the system. She knows a young woman on social assistance who keeps getting trained for various jobs—training paid for by the government—but she never sticks with the job she gets, or she gets fired from the job.

Here's someone who appears to be "milking the system" when likely there is something else going on that prevents her from succeeding.

More importantly, we should ask, *if one person or even a few people abuse the system, does that mean the whole system doesn't work?* Do the actions of one person mean no one else gets to benefit from the program? If seven or eight out of ten people are helped, do the two or three people who just can't manage to get their stuff together negate the evidence, the research, the anecdotes, the facts of success?

If seven or eight out of ten people are helped, why do we cancel a program because two or three can't cut it? If seventy or eighty percent of people are able to live and work with security and dignity, why do we insist the program isn't justifiable or feasible?

That's terrible math.

Do you know what a basic guaranteed income is *really* about? Forget the numbers, forget the math, and consider it from a human and humane perspective (because if we lose our humanity, we've lost everything): the basic guaranteed income—and Jesus' call for us to help people—is about hope.

Do *that* math: Help + Security + Dignity = Hope.

Poverty isn't something anyone seeks; no one *wants* to be poor. It happens because of biology—our brains and our bodies—and it happens because of the choices we or others make. It happens because of policies and prejudices, because of politicians and bureaucrats, because of educators and business owners and employees and …

Most people will not squander the chance to have a home, find work, finish school, and pay it forward. Most people will not squander the chance for their children to be better fed and clothed. Most people will not squander the chance to be hopeful, and thankful.

As a librarian named Dave Fletcher posted on social media, "I'd rather a poor person 'abuse the system' and end up with more than the bare minimum it takes to survive than a rich person abuse the system to make more money than anyone could ever need."[70]

We need to stop saying we can't do the math on this. We need to stop with the "learned helplessness" and instead take action. We need to stop doing things the way we've always done them. We need to stop thinking in ways that no longer serve us, or others. We need to stop limiting ourselves and our abilities and our potential.

We need to share our abundance.

We've heard again and again the new truth Jesus gives us. Now we need to *follow* the new way he showed us. Jesus asks us to love one another, to take care of one another, to help one another. Jesus says, "Come to me, you who are weary and carrying heavy burdens, and I will give you rest." I will give you a break from your worry and stress and despair. I will give you dignity and hope. I will give you a basic guaranteed income.

We are called to do what we can to help those who have less and struggle more. We are called to lift them up out of poverty, to help them help themselves, because "the poor" are not people outside our communities, they are among us—brothers and sisters and friends, the neighbors and strangers and enemies Jesus asked us to love. Jesus calls us to share their suffering, to alleviate their difficulties and marginalization, to restore their lost dignity and ensure their necessary social inclusion.

The subtitle of John Mighton's book claims that math is the key to a better world. Obviously, the world needs more math, *and* especially more Jesus.

THE ENCAMPMENT

It was dusk
when the couple arrived at the encampment
in the downtown park
the man carrying several bags
the woman heavily pregnant
and walking very slowly

renovicted from their apartment
told to go back where they came from
maybe they shouldn't be having a baby
if they couldn't afford rent plus utilities

A man in an orange reflective vest
hurried towards them
the couple asked if there was an extra tent
they could borrow
just for the night
just until her contractions started
and he shook his head
there was no room at the encampment
officials already making noise
about its size
surely a pregnant woman going into labor
would be the reason they were looking for
to shut it down

She felt the shift the moment she knew
they wouldn't make it to the hospital

Jesus in the World Today

An older woman standing in front of a tent
smoking a cigarette
waved the couple over
ducked into her tent
came back out with two tarps and some poles
with ropes attached
a blanket that smelled of smoke
she'd saved everything after someone had
an episode
wasn't sure if they'd be back
but the couple was welcome to it
for the night

the man carried the items to an empty space
near the fence
and the woman wept as he
spread a tarp on the ground
then the blanket on the tarp
so she could sit down

She felt the shift the moment she knew
this is where her baby would come into the world
in this encampment
surrounded by anxious strangers
a newborn cleaned with bottled water
and wrapped in a hoodie

as she pondered in her heart
how she could feel such joy
in such a lowly place
how she could feel such hope
when they had nothing

someone placed a bowl of warm soup in her hands
another wrapped a blanket around her shoulders
sheets appeared

The Encampment

with assurances they had been washed that day
a small flannel blanket a pair of socks
the miracle of a tiny knitted hat!

where did these gifts come from
the woman wondered as
someone whispered she'd been a nurse
and helped the woman
lay down on her side with a pillow between her knees

she felt the shift the moment she knew
the baby would be born
in this place safe and protected and loved
by anxious strangers

and she promised
the baby would know the story of those
who welcomed them when they were homeless
who fed them when they were hungry
who clothed him when he was naked
who visited him when he was born

her body shifted
and she heard her husband's voice
praying in the language of his heart
heard the voice murmuring into her ear
don't be afraid don't be afraid
she heard
the sound of angels
singing on the far side of the encampment

AFTER CHRISTMAS

Two days after a green but cold
Christmas
it started snowing
and Jesus gazed out the window at the
thickly falling
quickly accumulating
snow

then he drained the last mouthful of coffee
from his favorite Santa mug
and stepped away from the window

The dog
lying on his bed
raised his head

"Not yet, Pete," Jesus said

He turned to the low bookshelf next to his chair and
picked up each hand-carved piece of the nativity
wrapping them in cloth before putting them in the box
(the Magi weren't there
Pete having chewed them when he was a puppy)

He went to the small artificial tree
that stood on a table in the corner of his apartment and
began lifting each handmade ornament off the branches
wrapping them in cloth before putting them in the box

After Christmas

He lifted the angel from the top of the tree
and wrapped her in tissue paper
the angel was old and delicate
a gift from his first Christmas

After he folded up the tree and put it in its box
the dog raised his head

"Not yet, Pete," Jesus said

Jesus went to the kitchenette and
rinsed out his mug then wrapped it in bubble wrap
and placed it in the box with all the other decorations
he folded the box flaps together

Then he grabbed a bag of sliced bread
and made eight sandwiches from the meat
of the turkey he'd cooked two days earlier

He put the sandwiches in a cloth shopping bag
with chocolates and ginger cookies
gift cards from the fast-food restaurant
and a dozen pairs of wool socks

Jesus stood at the window of his apartment and
looked down at the snowy street
the streetlights at a nearby intersection
blinked red and green and yellow

The wind had come up
and the snow swirled

A person
wearing a long coat and several scarves
pushed a shopping cart filled with stuffed bags
along the snow-covered sidewalk
until getting stuck at the curb cut

JESUS IN THE WORLD TODAY

Pete got up from his bed and
put his front paws up on the window ledge
Jesus placed a hand on his dog's head
felt the coarse fur between Pete's ears
tickle the scar in his palm

"Let's go for a walk, Pete," Jesus said
"It's time for the work of Christmas to begin."

14. Build a Bigger Table

IF ASKED WHAT SYMBOL we associate with Jesus, we would likely answer "the cross." The cross is associated with the way Jesus died, and I reference his crucifixion through the scars in his hands in my poems. Yet this symbol makes me uncomfortable. Who wants to think about death by crucifixion, one of the most horrible ways to die? Who wants to be reminded that Jesus suffered that way?

According to Rev. Dr. Durrell Watkins, of Fort Lauderdale, Florida, "God did not want Jesus to suffer (God does not order, ordain, require or rejoice in torture). No, Jesus suffered because he wouldn't stay silent about the suffering of others."[71]

He wouldn't stay silent about the suffering of others is one of the best descriptions of Jesus I've discovered. Go and do likewise.

While I acknowledge that the cross, and the tomb for that matter, are significant symbols about resurrection, I prefer a symbol associated with Jesus' life and ministry, a symbol that reminds us to live as Jesus called us to live, to love as Jesus showed us to love. A symbol that reminds us that love is an action.

That symbol is the table: a common, ordinary item found in most homes, schools, churches, businesses. Every day, staff members, co-workers, students, families, adults and kids gather around a table to eat. They create a community every day at a table, even if only for a ten-minute snack.

We gather at tables. We come together at tables. To eat, to talk, to plan. To weep, to comfort, to find courage. To nourish the bodies and spirits of others and ourselves.

What better symbol for the purpose of Jesus' ministry than the table? What better way to unify people than with food? Nourishment for body and soul.

Theologian Diana Butler Bass posed this question a couple of years ago: "What if Christianity had focused its attention on Maundy Thursday's table instead of Good Friday's cross?"[72]

She goes on to say, in a very Jesusy, upside-down gospel kind of way that, "Perhaps the table is God's purpose and the cross was Rome's violent disruption?"

Whoa!

For Butler Bass, "Easter doesn't make violence redemptive, instead it proclaims the table as Good News."

Hold on, take a deep breath. Before you retreat into, "Hey, you can't change the way we think about Easter," remember that Jesus himself is a new way of thinking, acting, living, and believing. A new way and a new truth. Then and now. He continues to be relevant in the twenty-first century because he continues to challenge us to think in new ways.

Emily M. D. Scott, who wrote a book about creating worship that takes place with a meal, puts it this way: "Jesus gathered people around tables, but he also sent them out on roads. For every meal he shared, every drawing together around a heavy-laden table, there was a call to travel an unknown path. He sends us to figure it out as we go, teaching or healing or starting churches or just muddling through. Along the way, though, there are tables."[73]

We gather at the table to rejoice, renew, recalibrate, and rest. We connect and we come undone. We nourish and gather strength to go out again.

Here's what I love best about the table; it's associated with grace.

Grace sustains us to do the work of Jesus in the world, to have the courage and strength to be Jesus in the world today. And what is the expression of grace at the table but the expression of gratitude? We give thanks for the table and what it offers: food, fellowship, conversation, nourishment. Gratitude is our best spiritual practice, and where else do we give thanks and have the most reasons to be thankful than at the table?

Let us consider that the table—round or rectangle—is a place of hospitality, a place of welcome and inclusion. Dignity and compassion. Justice and peace. A chair, a space, a setting for everyone.

A place of love where everyone is equal and every meal is accessible.

The table gives us permission to follow Jesus with a focus on grace and redemption through our living right now.

There is a quote that circulates around the Internet every year at Thanksgiving: "When you have more than you need, build a longer table, not a higher fence."

And we'd ask, like Jesus would, *Who's at our table?* Not just, *Who's invited?*, but who comes in and sits down and eats whether they are invited or not? With whom are we breaking bread? For whom are we pouring wine? Who are we going *out* to invite *in*? Because the table, like Jesus, is about love.

"If we are to believe that the inclusive love of God is real, we'd better start building a bigger table," said author Kaitlin B. Curtice. "If we are truly to hold the space of *all tribes and tongues*—because the diversity of the world is included in the love of God—we'd better get to work breaking down systems of colonization wherever we find them."[74]

A great way to follow Jesus would be to do what Curtice suggests: look around to see who is poor, tired, and oppressed, then get rid of our doors and walls and even our dogma, and put those tables outside where they are accessible to everyone.

When I read that, I wrote "Woo hoo!" in the margin of my copy of her book. Amen would work, too.

In one of my first published pieces in a Canadian church magazine, I quoted someone as saying, "Burn the hymn books! Burn the pews!" This was early in my career as a freelance writer and I included that quote because it resonated with me personally. I forgot, however, to include enough context to prevent my interviewee from being confronted by people who objected to his statement.

I still think he's right, but better yet, tear out the pews and reconstruct them into tables. Reconstruct them into chairs. Take off the doors, take down the walls.

Sounds like dismantling the church building, doesn't it? But what's the point of having a table inside a church building if only a pre-approved few get the opportunity to sit at it?

Inviting Jesus to be present at our table means inviting everyone he loves. This is why, with Jesus, we always need a bigger table. This is why, for Jesus, we need to focus our attention on the table more than the cross.

BIRTHDAY PARTIES IN THE PARK

Jesus stood
on the path through the park
and listened

he heard birds chirping
leaves rustling in the breeze
and a dog barking

Pete lifted his head and sniffed the air

he heard the quiet smack of running shoes
on the well-worn asphalt path
as a woman jogged by
her blond ponytail swinging

He didn't hear
the usual sounds of the park
on a sunny Saturday afternoon

the giggles and shouts of children playing
the sizzle of food cooking on the outdoor grills
the loud music and the even louder calls and answers

Jesus walked along the path
until he reached the picnic area

the tables were empty
the grills were cold
and suddenly Jesus understood

Jesus in the World Today

there were no birthday parties at the park

no colorful tablecloths
no balloons bobbing in the breeze
no hammocks hanging between the sycamore trees

no brown-eyed black-haired children
running up to Pete chattering in Spanish
"Perro! Perro!"
holding out their hands so Pete could lick their fingers

no reason for Jesus to find a bench
in the shade of a tree and sit down
to watch as plates of food are set on the tables
and the children rush over
the teenagers appear
but the abuelas and abuelos
are served first

come to the table
eat drink
in remembrance of me
of us
of them

for one day we will be gone
there will be no more birthday parties in the park

I scream
you scream
we all scream
when ICE comes

WHO DO YOU SAY I AM?

Who do you say I am? Jesus asks

Fear says
You are unwelcome
You are a stranger
You are an abomination
You are unclean
You are an outsider
You are useless
You are too old
You are unlovable

Fear says
God doesn't love you
the way you are

Fear tells us terrible things are going to happen
Fear tells us we aren't going to be able to handle it
Fear tells us to go back where we came from
Fear tells us we don't belong here
Fear tells us we don't deserve to live

Fear starts talking as soon as we express any doubt
about humanity dignity responsibility humility
when we decide Jesus' command to love one another
doesn't apply in this situation to that person to those people

Fear loves when we doubt God's presence
Fear loves when we ignore Jesus' words

And yet
the good news is fear is a liar

If fear lies, what is the truth?

The truth is
you do not need to be afraid

Who do you say I am?

courage
audacity
passion
goodness
the way forward

What does the Lord require of you?
kindness, justice, and humility

What does the world need from you?
the world needs more Jesus

Fear lies and tells us to
deport the stranger
blame the poor
ignore the sick
feed the rich
love only thyself
give more to Caesar
throw lots of stones

Fear wants us to believe
that our faith is under attack
and we need to defend it from
the strangers, the poor, the sick, the meek, the peacemakers
women, immigrants, journalists, pro-choicers, liberals, socialists

Who Do You Say I Am?

What does the Lord require of you?
kindness, justice, and humility

Fear will tell us that is a lie
but we know
fear is a liar because

Jesus is the truth

15. Audacious Women

IN THE BOOK OF Proverbs, there is a collection of verses extolling the virtues of "a woman of valor."[75] As with so many literal readings of the Bible, this passage became the "instructions" for an obedient and traditional wife, but the original meaning referred to valor. Valor means bravery, courage, boldness, and audacity, so this is a woman of resourcefulness, compassion, wisdom, and strength. The Hebrew phrase is *Eshet Chayil*, "a woman of valor."[76]

There were many women of valor in Jesus' life, starting with his mother, Mary, and they all upheld the original meaning from Proverbs 31.

The deviation from the original meaning likely can be blamed on patriarchy. Patriarchy is a system of society or government in which men hold the power and women are mostly excluded from it; it has come to include the belief that men are created superior to women and therefore have authority over women.

In her 2013 book *Jesus Feminist*, Sarah Bessey announces that "Patriarchy is not God's dream for humanity."[77] I don't think there's a better description of what has gone wrong with our faith, and the world, than that.

Patriarchy is not the dream. Not the goal. Not the program. Not the way. Not the truth.

Instead, Bessey believes Jesus loves women on our own terms: "He treats us as equals to the men around him; he listens; he does not belittle; he honors us; he challenges us; he teaches us; he includes us—calls us beloved. Gloriously, this flies in the face of the cultural expectations of his time—and even in our own time."[78]

That's right. Jesus cared about the treatment and mistreatment of women. He didn't just include women in his ministry; he invited them and encouraged them. He stood up to those who would push them aside. He valued women and their contributions. He also saw how often they lived at the not-merciful mercy of men.

He wouldn't remain silent about the suffering of women.

In his book *The Rebel Christ*, Michael Coren says Jesus "is radical in his criticisms of divorce partly because of the sheer injustice involved, and of the pain, poverty, and disgrace it caused to women."[79]

To add insult to injustice, women were routinely written out of the stories about Jesus and his followers. Twenty-seven books make up the Christian scriptures, but only four are gospels about Jesus' life and ministry; seventeen are Paul's letters about Jesus the resurrected Christ, and there are eight other epistles, plus the book of Revelation.

All written by men. All chosen for inclusion in the Bible by men. By the early patriarchy.

Yet undeniably women were drawn to Jesus—the man, the teacher, the Messiah—quite possibly because he welcomed them and treated them as smart and capable even as they kept everyone clothed and fed (and probably insisted they stop and ask for directions because Thomas forgot the map again).

Patriarchy and its insufferable sense of entitlement—to land, to resources, to money, to women's bodies—is quite clearly not Jesus' dream for humanity.

Jesus' dream is love. Specifically, that all people live in peace, with respect and dignity, with their basic needs covered; that we all walk together with kindness, mercy, justice, and humility; that we build a larger table rather than a higher wall; that we unite instead of divide, regardless of gender, race, identity, age, and ability.

We've come a long way, baby, and there's still miles to go until we can rest.

Jesus lived in a very strict, patriarchal, religious society where women were considered property, more disposable and less valuable than any man. Women had little to no authority and were restricted to their husband's home, which was always in the husband's name. When it came to education, girls learned from their mothers at home, while males would have their formal education in the synagogue. Very few women were able to learn to read and write.

There were hundreds of laws, many of them purity laws, which Jesus broke many times as he went about doing what he had to do: touching, talking to, healing, and consoling people—rendering himself ritually unclean over and over again. It didn't seem to matter to him.

You can see how his actions would be particularly important to women who were not treated well by their fathers or husbands or families. Women were not treated well by their communities if their husbands died. Without the protection of a man, a woman was vulnerable, even doomed. You can see how women who were poor, sick, abandoned, and at risk would be drawn to this man who blessed them.

Miraculously, considering how rigorously some religious leaders tried to remove women from documents—and in the case of Pope Gregory, change a woman's identity so as to disparage and discredit her—we know that women played a pivotal role in the life and ministry of Jesus (who was, remember, a devout Jew, with a strong streak of social justice and common sense).

We are familiar with Jesus' mother, Mary, and with Mary Magdalene, who was *not* a prostitute; yet there are two other women in the Christian scriptures who deserve special mention because of what was done to them by the patriarchy. These two women deserve special mention because we can be encouraged and motivated by their bravery and fortitude in following Jesus.

Junia served alongside Paul in his ministry and was imprisoned because of that work. You've never heard of Junia, the female apostle? That's likely because only male apostles were acknowledged and written about, and Junia suffered a similar fate as Mary Magdalene, whose identity was altered to suit the purposes of the early church councils, one of which was to create a patriarchal line of leadership.

Apparently, in later translations of Paul's letter that mentions Junia, an "s" was added to the end of her name, making it into a masculine form. Except that Junia was a common female name and there was no male equivalent—there was no Junias! Was it an honest mistake or yet another attempt to strip women of their status as followers of Jesus? Did some translator just make up a name in order to "disappear" a woman from the texts? Recently, experts have acknowledged that the name is definitively feminine.

Then there was Thecla, who also hung out with Paul. I learned about her from Meggan Watterson, author of *Mary Magdalene Revealed*. It's an incredible story. Thecla heard Paul's preaching and ran away from home (and a pending marriage) to be a Jesus follower. She saved herself from being burned to death for leaving her fiancé, from being raped, and from a lion attack, after which she jumped into a pit of water and declared herself baptized in the name of Jesus Christ.

Many of us in the twenty-first century don't know this story about Thecla, but, to early Christians, this girl who baptized herself was well-known. The "Acts of Paul and Thecla" was a popular read back in the second century. According to the book, which was written after her time, Thecla lived to be 90, unmarried and childless, after ministering and healing in the name of Jesus the rest of her life. She was considered a symbol of freedom and empowerment for women.

Watterson writes that Thecla, "did what her heart was telling her to do. And this was the sacrilege to those in power. That she refused to obey or validate any authority outside of her. Even Paul's. She baptized herself because she realized she could. She realized that all along, within her, she contained the power to save herself."[80]

She followed her heart, and her heart told her to follow Jesus. She believed she could do it and she did. She persisted.

Women of early Christianity—whether Mother Mary, Martha and Mary, Mary Magdalene, or Junia, Thecla, Phoebe the deacon, Lydia the patron, or Priscilla the first preacher—all were encouraged and supported and nurtured as disciples of Jesus and ministers of his new way. All were tough and tenacious and resilient. And most of them get overlooked because Paul's words are so much easier to twist into misinformation.

In *The Making of Biblical Womanhood,* historian, professor and pastor's wife Beth Allison Barr wrote about staying silent in the face of unjust scriptural justifications:

> I knew the truth about Paul's women. I knew the reality that women who are praised in the Bible—like Phoebe, Priscilla, and Junia—challenge the confines of modern biblical womanhood. As a historian, I knew that women were kept out of leadership roles in my own congregation because Roman patriarchy had seeped back into the early church. Instead of ditching pagan Rome and embracing Jesus, we had done the opposite—ditching the freedom of Christ and embracing the oppression of the ancient world.[81]

Do you see how everything comes back to Jesus and his dream for humanity? His dream was certainly not one that treated women—and others—as second-class citizens, as not worthy, as sinners, as savages, as "less than." He wanted us to create a community, a world, built on love, and he wanted people to come together, to be unified. Regardless of gender, race, identity, age, and ability.

Jesus encouraged his disciples to maintain their unity after his death. That is the new way Jesus sought for all his disciples, the men and the women who followed him and would, he hoped, carry on his ministry and create his new vision for the world. A world that included—named and celebrated, welcomed and respected—women.

You know how I like to bring Jesus into the world today? Let's channel courageous Thecla these days, too; Thecla, that symbol of freedom and empowerment for women. She was a supersized woman of valor, one who came to embody the "shameless audacity" Jesus suggests is needed to get what we need—and to hang on to what we have already achieved.

May we all be as audacious as Thecla in following Jesus and in claiming our right to choose the life we want.

REMINDERS

Jesus placed his items on the counter
two toothbrushes
two tubes of toothpaste
two packages of soap
two tubes of hand sanitizer
and two large fruit and nut chocolate bars

every item he buys for himself
he buys one to give away
this time for
the man living under the bridge near the park
where Jesus walks his dog

there is a bin of wool-blend socks
next to the counter
and he adds two pairs
he doesn't need any more socks
but they are on sale
he'll give away both

He holds out two twenty-dollar bills
and the cashier takes them
pauses
then looks into his eyes

"We have a cream that can reduce the look of
your scars,"
she says with a nod at his hand

Jesus in the World Today

Jesus smiles
"Thank you but I'm fine."

"It's not that expensive," she says

Jesus nods
"I'm fine."

"Wouldn't you rather not be reminded
of what happened to you?" she insists

"It's not me who needs to be reminded,"
Jesus answered

The woman turns away
to ring in his cash
then counts out his change
placing the coins
gently into the center of
his outstretched palm

his scars
the currency of
being human

16. Who Are You Looking For?

IF THERE IS ONE thing about Christianity, about our faith as followers of Jesus, if there is one thing we know and one thing we've never quite grasped as we built our churches and designed our vestments and created our liturgies, it's that Jesus was not a king. Jesus was not a lord. Jesus was not a president or a general or a CEO.

He was a carpenter and a travelling preacher. He was a teacher and a friend. He might even have been a lover.

And without winning an election or taking over a bunch of companies or networking (and bribing) his way into a Very Important Position, he did this amazing, incredible, awesome, transforming, radical thing, this new thing. He showed us how to live a good life.

He showed us how to be brave and kind, courageous and compassionate. He showed us how to do what is right, and to do it sometimes with passion and anger. He showed us how to endure the suffering that may come with doing the right thing.

He gave us the truth about life, about living, and he showed us how to do it.

Us. Ordinary, everyday, common people. People who fish. People who weave. People who bake and cook and feed others. People who are farmers and mechanics. People who run inns and build furniture. People who go to church and school and the library. People who sit in arenas or on bleachers or stand along a wall watching their kids participate in some kind of sport.

Why do we ignore the truth he gave us and the way he showed us? Why do we want the crown and the purple robe—the vestments used to mock Jesus as he was brought before the crowd chanting, "Crucify him!"? Why do we want him to be a king?

Who are you looking for?

Let's consider the man who took ordinary bread and common wine and transformed it into a remembrance of his teachings, of his final command: Love each other as I have loved you. The man who created communion: come, eat and drink; you are welcome at the table.

Table. Bread. Wine. Nothing fancy. Nothing specially made. Just the furniture and food and beverage of ordinary, common people.

Us. You and me. And them. And those people.

Who are you looking for?

Jesus asks this question twice during his final days: Once, when the police, soldiers, and religious leaders come to the garden of Gethsemane after the meal with his disciples; and then again when he finds Mary crying at the empty tomb.

Who are you looking for?

A savior? A miraculous healer? A death-defying god?

But we know we don't get what we want—we get what we need.

We get the man who insists there's a better, more equitable way to live; who is prepared to die for this belief; who is entombed; and who appears as a vision to Mary, then later to his friends and followers to reassure them that love doesn't die. The truth cannot be killed. They can go on without him if they love one another as he showed them how to love.

We get the ordinary, everyday, common man, who is just like us; who does this amazing, incredible, awesome, transforming, radical, new thing. He transformed death into life. An end into a beginning. Fear into love. Grief into hope.

Who are you looking for?

When we are looking for Jesus, do we ever look on the sidelines, in the shadows, in the poor neighborhoods where there are no sidewalks or streetlights, in the prisons and safe injection sites, in the waiting room of the mental health clinic?

When we are looking for Jesus, do we ever feel uncomfortable, out of our element, as if we stick out from the crowd, don't fit in; do we feel conspicuous, afraid, but somehow want to keep on doing what we are doing because it feels like the right thing?

When we are looking for Jesus, do we see him in an ordinary place and in the common opportunity, in the space that opens between us when we make a connection?

Maybe he's the cashier at the grocery store. Maybe he's the janitor at the elementary school. Maybe he's the nurse on the night shift at the hospital. Maybe he's the person mowing your lawn. Maybe he's the person looking back at you in the mirror.

Jesus did this amazing, incredible, awesome, transforming, radical, new thing for us. For *us*. Who are as ordinary and everyday and common as he was; it's just that he trusted in God and in himself and in his purpose; he trusted in his own heart far more than we do.

Jesus doubted and did what he did anyway. Jesus doubted and said what he said anyway. He was a troublemaker and a peacemaker. He was politically subversive and radically inclusive. And I like to think he had a dry wit that most modern readers of the Bible don't get.

We never quite get Jesus, do we?

We want a show of power but we get the man who walks humbly. We want a show of force but we get the man who talks about loving our enemies. We want a freedom fighter but we get the man who rides a donkey. We want a death-defying savior but we get the man who dies by crucifixion.

This is very confusing.

"Who are you looking for?" Jesus asks Mary as they meet outside the empty tomb.

It's a moment full of hope and joy, revelation and renewal, possibility and potential. Full of love.

Who do you say I am?

And why are you looking for me?

WERE YOU THERE

Where were you when they crucified
my Lord?

I tried to cry out for help
but my face was pressed into the asphalt
by the knee in my neck
as people recorded my pain on their phones

Were you there when they crucified
my Lord?

I held the arm of an elderly Ukrainian woman
as she climbed over the concrete remains
of a bridge bombed the day before
as we walked towards the border

Were you there when they crucified
my Lord?

I opened the door to Taliban fighters
when they banged on the door
with the butt of their guns
and I lied about my daughter hiding
in a room at the back of the house

Were you there when they crucified
my Lord?

I waited at the airport in Yemen
for a plane carrying food and water

but it never arrived
and I returned empty-handed
to the children suffering malnutrition

Were you there when they crucified
my Lord?

I was arrested in Texas
while eating supper with my child
who had just started taking hormones
to begin their transition
they wore the earrings I gave them
the day after they told me their true identity

Were you there when they crucified
my Lord?

I traveled through northern Gaza
with people who would cook hot meals
for Palestinians struggling to survive
in the rubble of bombed buildings
but we didn't make it
because a missile slammed into our vehicle

Were you there when they crucified
my Lord?

I stood in the crowded emergency room
at the only hospital still open in that county
as a heavily-pregnant woman cried out in pain
while another woman in a pantsuit
explained she wasn't covered for a C-section

Were you there when they crucified
my Lord?

Jesus in the World Today

My hands
my feet
my side
my forehead
bear the scars of
your absence
your silence
your ignorance
your viciousness
your vote

Where were you when they crucified
my Lord?

IN THE GARDEN

There is a walled garden
inside the city under siege
the trees bare-limbed in the early spring
the grass brown and scrubby
the soil damp

and everything—
the gardens and shrubs
the walkways and benches
the top of the stone walls –
are covered in a thin layer of
ash
and dust
mixed with blood and tears

Jesus pushes through the gate
which creaks and hangs open
after he passes through
his dog, Pete, padding along behind him
close to his calves
scenting the worst of humanity
that his person can't smell
just sense
through the soles of his feet
and the scars in his palms

Sitting down on a bench
Jesus looks up
at the blue sky
and listens

for birds singing –
because hope is the thing with feathers
he once read—
but all he hears is the
waxing and waning wail of
an air raid siren

Pete lies down at his feet
and rests his chin
on the ground
feels the shock wave
from the explosion of a bomb
hitting a school
a hospital
an apartment building

Jesus looks down at his hands
flexes them open and closed
then clasps them together
leans his elbows on his knees
and closes his eyes

"I am filled with sorrow,"
he says,
"and my heart is troubled."

In the distance
a rumbling

"I'm holding the world's cup of suffering,
the first to drink from it,
and the last."

A few streets away
the sound of gunshots

In the Garden

"I know this is not what you want
yet here we are
again,
our cups of pain
overflowing."

On the other side of the wall
voices shouting

Pete lifts his head
sits up
lays his chin on Jesus' knee

Jesus strokes his dog's head
and sighs

"Those who use bombs
die by bombs."

Jesus walks to the gate
and looks beyond the garden
at the black smoke and orange flames

"The time has come,"
he says to Pete,
and together they walk up the street
to the theater where he's heard
citizens
civilians
children
are seeking shelter
praying they are safe

17. Just Say Yes

THERE ARE SOME BOOKS you read that make you hold them to your chest and sigh, "Where have you been all my adult life?" Bono's nearly 600-page memoir, published in 2022 and titled *Surrender: 40 Songs, One Story*, was one of those books for me.

Bono is the lead singer of the Irish rock group U2, a group that has been together for 40 years. They released their first seven albums in the 1980s, when I was in high school. They gave us great songs like "I Still Haven't Found What I'm Looking For," "With or Without You," and "Pride (In the Name of Love)."

Although I can sing along with their songs, I have to admit I wasn't really into U2 as a teenager. My go-to UK band was The Police with leader singer Sting.

A few years ago, however, my best friend mentioned that Bono had done some interviews about the Psalms and when I was searching for quotes for a previous book and found something Bono said that suited my needs, I became intrigued about his social justice work.

How could I have gone 40 years without knowing that the lead singer of one of the most famous rock bands in the world believes the world needs more Jesus? Who says that songs are his prayers? I now refer to his book as *The Gospel According to Bono*.

Bono says he'll always be first up for an altar call. "If I was in a café right now and someone said, 'Stand up if you're ready to give your life to Jesus,' I'd be the first to my feet," he writes.[82]

Wow. How many of us would do the same, be the first to our feet if asked, "Are you ready to follow Jesus right now?" What does it take to say Yes to Jesus? To say yes to love, to justice, to mercy, to peace?

It certainly takes surrender. As Bono writes, "It's an extraordinary thing, the moment of surrender."

Here's the thing about surrender. It's not about giving up. It's not waving the white flag. It's not capitulating or chickening out or bailing. Surrender is about giving in. It's about yielding, submitting, accepting. It's about taking on something or someone. It's about saying Yes.

You stop resisting and say Yes. You stop finding reasons to say no and just say Yes.

Yes to doing the right thing, even when it's hard.

Yes to loving your neighbor, even when they're rude.

Yes to being vocal about who you love, who you support, who is welcome in your life, in your home, in your church.

Pentecost, celebrated as the "birthday of the Christian church," is all about saying yes to the Holy Spirit. After all, this event is all about the Holy Spirit. The story goes like this: These early followers of the Jesus way were just hanging out when all of a sudden the wind picked up and rattled every window. That wind blew in what looked like tongues of fire that came to rest above each person. They were filled with the Holy Spirit and began to speak all sorts of languages which gave them the ability to communicate Jesus' law of love to everyone.[83]

What I love about this story is the reminder that what we need already exists within us. The Spirit is already at work within us because, as another story goes, Jesus had already breathed the Holy Spirit into his friends.[84] If we follow Jesus, our hearts are already burning inside us[85] with that hot, holy, energetic passion for peace, love, and understanding.

"We think the Spirit is with us when we feel good," wrote Rev. Dr. Racheal Keefe on her blog. "We choose not to remember the unsettling capacity of the Spirit to discomfort the comfortable and lead us to places we would not go on our own."[86]

Listen, that's what happened when I wrote my first Jesus poem. It was like a little flame danced above my head. And look where that has taken me. Could this be discipleship? Out of my comfort zone? Yikes!

When habit and ritual become by rote, without thinking or feeling, noticing or reacting; when the comfort zone becomes so comfortable there's no room to grow or expand; that's when we need someone with enthusiasm, with passion, with a burning heart to come in and shake things up.

But what if no one says Yes to the shake up? What if no one stands up with you?

I think it's safe to say that the church is not the first place we think of when we talk about cutting-edge change. The mainline church—generally speaking—isn't a big fan of change. Of doing things differently. Of opening up to new ideas.

For some reason, we have a hard time saying Yes to Jesus and to what he'd like us to do.

We say, "Well, it's my turn to host the fellowship hour after worship so …"

And we say, "The worship services for the next two months are already planned so…"

We also say things like, "We haven't seen you in church for a while"; and "You know, we have a really nice nursery where you and your baby could stay during the worship."

Here's a big one: "This is the way we've always done it."

And another: "We'll always have poor people."

If someone said, "Stand up if you're ready to follow Jesus," would each one of us stand right up and say, "Yes," or would we look down at our laps to avoid eye contact, look around to see if anyone else is standing up, anyone we want to do this with?

Why do we hold back? What are we afraid of?

That's a lot of questions. How Jesusy of me. Apparently, Jesus asked 307 questions. Questions like, *Who do you say I am? Do you want to get well? Why did you doubt? Why are you afraid?*

Of course Jesus, being Jesus, didn't typically ask Yes or No questions. Yet everything Jesus asks of us can be answered not with words but with action. With love. With kindness, mercy, justice, compassion, fairness, equity, hospitality, acceptance, and

Just Say Yes

inclusion. With food for body and spirit. With bread and wine for community and connection.

With welcome and wonder and the question *what if*.

So that windy, fiery moment that became known as Pentecost (which means "fifty" in Greek, for the fiftieth day after Easter) is really the beginning of the journey of saying Yes to being led to places we would not go on our own.

We need to go with Jesus.

Pentecost reminds us to get windy and fiery, and to give the world more Jesus. Before you panic and start patting your head to put out the flames in case someone sees you and knows your heart said Yes to Jesus, "giving the world more Jesus" just means…

When Jesus says, "Love one another," we say Yes.

When Jesus says, "Treat others as you want to be treated," we say Yes.

When Jesus says, "Love your enemies," we say Yes.

When Jesus says, "You are the light of the world," we say Yes.

When Jesus says, "Turn the other cheek, give up your coat as well, go another mile, help your neighbor," we say Yes.

When Jesus says, "Seek, knock, ask, pray, forgive, take the hard road, wash feet, break bread, build a bigger table, and do it all with shameless audacity," we say Yes.

We say Yes to places that take us out of our comfort zone, but where the law of love is the way: Love God, love your neighbors, love your enemies. Love as I loved.

To be a follower of Jesus means to be transformed by grace and empowered by Spirit—the creative, abundant, unstoppable, unquenchable Spirit; the fuel for the fire in our burning hearts, for the flames lighting our minds on fire and illuminating the path we need to take.

What are we going to do with that energy? Are we going to be afraid? Are we going to hesitate, overthink, hide? Or are we going to say Yes? Even if we are afraid. Even if, or perhaps especially if, it's going to take us to places where we would not go on our own but where Jesus wants us to go. The places where we need to be.

Just say yes. Because, according to the "Gospel of Bono," Love is bigger than anything in its way.[87]

CONSIDER THE ICE CREAM CONE

Jesus sits in the park by the harbor
on a bench in the leafy shade of a maple tree
he slips off his sandals
and places his hot feet on the cool blades of grass

He holds an ice cream cone in one hand
a swirl of purple and yellow and bright blue
melting in the summer heat

Jesus is inordinately delighted by ice cream
had planned to work his way through
the long list of flavors inside the store
in this quiet seaside village
but this is his third time choosing Moon Mist*
because there's something about
the combination of colors
something in the way
they each have their own taste
yet unify into one delicious experience
that makes him happy
makes him forget the troubles of the day

"Consider the ice cream in this cone,"
Jesus says (to no one in particular
although one seagull glances his way)
"It simply exists as ice cream.
See how it sits in the plain cone and is content
doesn't yearn for sprinkles
or long to be wrapped in a waffle.
See how it melts yet doesn't resist its melting.

Consider the Ice Cream Cone

It is eaten—"
he licks the dribbles around the cone—
"or it melts and gets wiped away.
The ice cream does not worry about what happens to it."

A drip of ice cream
falls onto his white shirt
the splash of purple and yellow and bright blue
lays there on the cotton
"No worries! Life is about more than food and clothes,"
Jesus says,
licking the ice cream and watching seagulls
circle slowly over the calm water

* *Moon Mist ice cream flavors are grape, banana, and bubblegum, and only available in Atlantic Canada.*

18. Part of Jesus' Family

IN 2018, I ATTENDED a ceremony in a small rural town that was raising a Pride flag on one of its flagpoles for the first time.

I was there because I know one of the co-chairs of the county's Pride committee. I know his journey and how hard he's worked to accept not only himself but also to accept the fact he was rejected by members of his former church.

I was there because that symbol of tolerance, acceptance, and safety matters to a lot of people I know—some I call friends, some I call family. I was there because I remember what happened thirty years earlier.

In 1988, The United Church of Canada fielded the idea of ordaining male and female clergy who were gay. It became this heated and divisive debate that ended with some people leaving the denomination in anger while others formed a group called "Community of Concern" to resist the final decision that supported the ordination of all members of the church, regardless of sexual orientation.

With that decision, The United Church of Canada became the first and only mainstream Christian church in Canada to affirm that openly gay and lesbian people are eligible for ordination, because of their faith in Jesus, their commitment to his way, his truth and his life. Because they were people of faith who had heard God's call to spiritual service.

On the subject of same-sex relationships, Michael Coren, author of *The Rebel Christ*, says Jesus didn't mention the subject. He believes Jesus "didn't really have an opinion on the subject as it applies to the modern world. I am more convinced, however, that he didn't condemn it and that Christians have gotten this wrong for far too long."[88] Coren emphasizes Jesus' call to love and to accept.

There are over 2,000 verses in the Bible about poverty. About money. About the rich and the poor. The verses in both the Hebrew and Christian scriptures that are quoted as condemning homosexuality don't actually say anything about same-sex relationships. They address promiscuity, idolatry, overindulgence—the spiritual, not physical kind.[89] People have had to work very hard to use the scriptures, particularly Paul's writings, to *misinterpret the original Greek words* in order to allow them to judge, discriminate against, and encourage intolerance towards people who identify as LGBTQIAS2+.

When the ordination debate was raging in my church, I was 18 years old. I listened to people talk, I read about what the issues were, I heard people's "Absolutely not!" responses and also the wishes of those who were gay and lesbian who simply wanted to follow what they believed was their calling—to become faith leaders in their church as well as be spouses and partners and parents.

None of that made as big an impact on my life as what I heard from my own mother. We were driving somewhere and apparently what was going on in the church, what she was hearing at meetings, was troubling her heart. Suddenly she said to me, "If you were to come to me and tell me you were a lesbian, it wouldn't matter. I wouldn't want to lose you. It wouldn't matter to me. I would love you no matter what."

That's a pretty powerful statement for a parent to make. She really couldn't know if I was a lesbian or not. I mean, I'd been "boy crazy" since I was five years old but hey, that could have just been me doing what was expected, hiding my true identity with a lot of boyfriends.

It didn't matter to her. She loved me and would continue to love me no matter what.

Which sounds exactly like Jesus' call to love and to accept.

Thinking of that conversation now, I could ask *Where was Jesus in that scenario?*

I grew up with those words of love and acceptance in my mind and heart, knowing that no matter who I was, who I loved, or what I did, my family would not reject me. My family would love me. My mother's words echoed the most significant and transformative and radically amazing grace about Jesus' ministry; it is based on love, on compassion, mercy, fairness, justice, and inclusion.

Jesus died for that ministry, but we've done a poor job carrying on his mission.

It's not Jesus standing in a pulpit in a church full of white middle-class people on a Sunday morning, cherry-picking the most hurtful and judgmental quotes from the Bible.

It's not Jesus in the coffee shop with the other "Christians" going on about how "those people" are ruining traditional family values.

Where is Jesus in that scenario? Since the values that mattered to Jesus were compassion and tolerance and mercy, he would be standing outside the women's bathroom at the mall with a 12-year-old raised as a boy and now identifying as a girl, telling her he loves her just as she is, that in God's eyes she is precious as she is, not as she was born, but as she is as a person—whoever that person is.

Just as he stood by the lepers and the epileptics—those shunned by everyone else as diseased and demonic—Jesus would stand by those who are persecuted for not being "like us," who are persecuted by their so-called "Christian family."

Jesus set the example for standing with those who are oppressed, who are judged by their peers, who are shunned and tormented. Jesus calls us to love them, to welcome them and whoever else walks a path that other don't understand. Jesus asks us to choose compassion and acceptance and justice over fear and ignorance and hatred. Jesus gave his life for that request because he would not remain silent about the suffering of others. He gave his life for what he believed. And he believed that he was showing us the way, the truth, and the life.

This is precisely why we need more Jesus in the world. We need the radical ministry of Jesus to remind each of us that we are all worthy of love.

Part of Jesus' Family

What makes Jesus' ministry so radical and so needed is that he chose to hang out with people mainstream society rejects, those who feel the love of God even when the rest of the "Christian family" persecutes them, those who shake up the establishment.

Because that's who truly needs him. Those who struggle.

I've never struggled. And I had my mother's words to make me feel protected and accepted and safe all my life.

The stakes are higher now. Not for me, but for my friend.

The young man who invited me to the Pride flag raising was raised as a girl, came out as gay in high school, but realized before graduation his true identity. As soon as he moved away to university, he began the transition. It's not easy doing any of that in a small, rural community.

He told me that his "Christian family" rejected him when he revealed his truth. He was devastated, but here's the amazing grace of his story: once he started university, once he began to live true to himself, away from that church and the people who had rejected him, *he still felt God tugging at his heart.*

This is why his story matters. Because it didn't matter what that *church* thought about his authentic self, *he* knew God loved him and wanted him in this world. He realized he is precious to God as he is, not as he was born but as he is as a person.

He still felt God tugging at his heart. Those are the most powerful and transformative words I've heard since my mother spoke to me in the car many decades ago. Despite the way "Christians" treated him, despite his exile from the church community in which he'd grown up—my friend didn't feel rejected by God.

That's huge. That's the proof. The proof of the power of love.

And the proof that Jesus has the right idea.

Victoria Loorz, founder of Church of the Wild and the author of the book by the same name, wrote, "Is it possible to change the world by love alone? We are already kin. So, yes, I believe that only love can prevail against the unraveling we are facing."[90]

We are already kin. All of us are part of Jesus' family and we are loved no matter what. We are loved, all of us, just as we are when we answer the call for kindness, justice, and humility.

Here's the only question we need to ask when we are confronted with an idea or a request that makes us feel uncomfortable, or when we meet someone who is walking a path different from ours: Is God tugging at *my* heart right now?

SON OF MAN'S BEST FRIEND

Jesus hoisted the straps of the backpack
up and over his shoulders

"Pete," he said to his dog,
standing next to him at the start of the trail
"Next time, don't pack so many balls."

Jesus laughed out loud at his own joke

Pete was not a dog who chased balls
or sticks or cats or other dogs
not even squirrels

Pete was the kind of dog who liked
to stand back
keep an eye on what other people were doing
who preferred his own company
to the company of others

Oh, sure, Pete was friendly
approachable in that shaggy dog of mix breeding
kind of way that made everyone feel comfortable
he welcomed everyone who wandered over
to talk to Jesus
let them pet his head
and feed him snacks

but left to his own devices
(he really was the kind of dog
you could do that with
just let him do his own thing)

Jesus in the World Today

Pete was more apt to find a nice wide rock
to stand on
so he could look around
get the lay of the land
smell the air
see what was what
and who was who

Afterall,
it wasn't easy being Jesus' dog
Jesus tended to wander off
lost in his own thoughts
distracted by people needing assistance
people who reached out to him
called his name invited him to join them
that happened a lot

once they were on their way to the friendship center
to help clean graffiti off their outside wall
and somehow they ended up
walking in a parade instead

and somehow Pete ended up wearing
a rainbow bandana
with pink and blue ribbons fluttering from his tail

another time
Pete spent a couple of days at the animal shelter
because Jesus had come across someone
who had overdosed
and until the police figured out
Jesus didn't have anything to do with it
had just stayed with the man until
the paramedics brought him back to life
they'd kept Jesus in lockup

Son of Man's Best Friend

Pete shook off the memory
the shelter was
loud and noisy and uncomfortable
he wished he could convince everyone they met
to be angels and release those poor dogs
from their prison

he stopped to snuffle his nose in some moss
at the side of the trail
before running to catch up to Jesus
who was heading uphill

like there was a reason he had to reach the top
in a hurry

19. Healing Touch, Healing Tears

THREE DAYS AFTER MY mother had surgery to remove cancerous polyps in her colon, I was scheduled to read the scripture at church.

Mum's recovery in hospital was going well so I went ahead with the reading, which was from chapter five of the Gospel of Mark, the story of the woman with chronic hemorrhaging who touched Jesus' robe and was healed.

Now, I choke up pretty easily and I have had to pause in my delivery of a message to collect myself because sometimes my passion makes me emotional. Still, I have never sobbed my way through a message or prayer. That's what happened, however, as I read verse 34, "Daughter, your faith has made you well. Go in peace and be healed of your disease."[91]

As soon as my brain saw that line and connected it with what was going on with my mother, I started to cry. I had absolutely no control over my thoughts or my tear ducts. No one came to my rescue so I just kept reading—and crying—to the last verse.

During the prayers of the people, someone offered up my mother's name and a murmur of understanding flowed through the congregation. Afterwards, a few people thanked me for making them hear that scripture in a new way.

My mother was in hospital with cancer and my father was living in the locked unit at a nursing home because of early-onset dementia. Yet that was the first time I'd cried during a time when I was holding it all together for everyone else. It was a healing moment for me.

Many years later, I was asked to give the message for my community's ecumenical World Day of Prayer gathering. I had to read another story about healing and, fortunately, there was no crying this time. It's the story about the healing pool whose waters were believed to be stirred by an angel. According to the story, when the waters were stirred, the first person into the pool after that would be cured of whatever afflicted them. Stopping by on his way to Jerusalem, Jesus spoke to a person who had, apparently, lounged poolside for more than three decades, waiting to be cured.

Jesus asked the man, "Do you want to get well?"

When the person replied that no one would help him into the water after it was stirred, Jesus replied rather curtly, "Get up! Pick up your mat and walk."[92]

The man was immediately healed, picked up his mat, and walked off.

In this story, Jesus does not say, "You are healed." Rather, he asks a question: "Do you want to get well?" Did Jesus cure him? Or heal him? It's an important distinction, especially if we want to walk the Jesus walk.

First, there is a difference between healing and curing. Curing means "eliminating all evidence of disease," while healing means "becoming whole"—even if what afflicts you remains.

Historian and theologian John Dominic Crossan said, "What I see Jesus doing when he heals people is bringing them into a new community. He takes in people who may see themselves as a burden or an embarrassment."[93]

You can be healed without being cured. That happens when you are surrounded by people who love you and care for you, who support you and help you. Who accept you just as you are, whatever shape you're in for whatever reason.

Just like Jesus did.

Healing is about bringing people into a new kind of community where they are not an embarrassment or a burden, where they are not simply ignored and stepped over, but where they are welcomed and accepted and included, and supported to be themselves and to live their lives.

Doing that—giving people a place where they feel at home, at rest, where they feel they can be themselves no matter what is going on with their minds or bodies—helps them pick up their mats and walk. Just as they are. To do what they are supposed to do.

Jesus must have seen something in the person at the edge of the pool that the person couldn't see in themselves. Perhaps the person had just given up. But Jesus realized that with encouragement, with a community to support him, the person could be "healed."

Healing is a two-way street: realizing your own potential to heal yourself; and using your skills, your holy energy, to offer healing to others. Healing is an exchange of courage.

Healing is an act of love.

According to pastor and author Nadia Bolz-Weber, this is how Jesus works: "Seeing us. Offering the truth. Restoring what is broken. Pursuing our healing long after we've given up. Loving us into wholeness. And wanting us to be made new, to be made whole, to take up our mats and walk."[94]

That is how Jesus' encounter with the person at the pool, his encounter with the blind man on the side of the road, with the woman in the crowd who touches his robe, are all about healing, which is about love and compassion and mercy and justice.

More importantly, being healed by Jesus becomes a call to be a healer yourself. To pay it forward. To welcome and include and reconcile. And make new.

We are called to get up from our mats, to get off the couch, put down our phones, and use our skills—our voices and our energy—to heal ourselves, each other, and the world. To do what we feel called to do—because love is an action.

Make no mistake. Sometimes helping others pick up their mat and walk into wellness takes every bit of heart, mind, soul, and strength that we have. Sarah Bessey said, "There are a lot of institutions, powers, principalities, and yes, evil that benefit from us giving up hope. They lick their chops at our despair and work to make us feel powerless. To keep us in the cycle of outrage and ineffective complacency. To fool us into thinking that there is no possibility of healing, our small agency isn't enough, our voices don't count, our community too divided."[95]

Healing is an act of hope. I see you; I will help you pick up your mat and walk.

Healing is not about curing a disease; it's not about finding a solution for a problem. Healing is about being able to live with our illnesses and issues, our diseases and disabilities because of the support of others.

This is why Jesus reminds us over and over about "the poor." Viewing the world through the lens of healing and reconciliation means we are called to accept and include and support those who live in poverty, appreciating that many people live in poverty because of health issues.

We aren't called to "cure" a person's physical and psychological challenges but to offer healing to those living with them.

We are called to help others "pick up their mats and walk." To offer unconditional, non-judgmental support and encouragement and resources so that they can live as well as they can; so that by their faith—but also by policies and programs- they can be healed.

Jesus offers us the possibility of personal transformation—the possibility to heal ourselves and realize our potential—which leads to social transformation as we offer healing to others, the world, and realize the potential of all humanity to live in harmony with each other.

This is huge!

Here's another thing: When someone reaches out and touches us, we are called to offer healing right then and there. Not just or only when it's convenient for us. Not when it's a good time. Not when it's private and there aren't so many people around; when you're not so busy. When someone reaches out and touches us knowing we have what they need to be healed, we respond immediately.

This is all such amazing grace. Bringing people out of their dark tombs of worry and pain and isolation to find a light-filled space welcoming them. Come in and sit down. Find sanctuary.

Find comfort and support. Find love. And through those things, feel included, sustained. Healed.

"So what are you doing with your one wild and precious life?" asked Mary Oliver,[96] who I believe was a manifestation of Jesus through her poetry. What are you going to do with your one healed and holy life?

At the end of that World Day of Prayer service, a woman who has lived with multiple sclerosis for years thanked me for my message. I don't remember exactly what she said, but the idea that you can be healed through love, through care and inclusion, even if your illness can't be cured, was deeply meaningful to her. She believed she had experienced that in her community.

That almost made me cry.

HEALING IN THE STREETS

(Inspired by verse 3 of the hymn, "Jesus Christ Is Waiting," by John L. Bell)

Jesus, mercy-provider,
we seek healing for the wounds
of our own crucifixions,
all the ways we
break hearts
wound bodies
shatter spirits
fragment minds
with words, with actions,
with silence, with complacency,
with intentional misinformation,
with policies and laws.

We pray to you for healing
but in reality, we just want our problems to go away
we want to feel well, we want to end our suffering,
we want to seal up the cracked parts
and glue together all the broken bits,
we want our lives to be perfect
just by praying.

Jesus, justice-seeker,
we know fairness and mercy and humility
are the ways to walk through this world,
wherever we are, with whomever we meet,
yet we act as if offering kindness
is akin to walking barefoot on broken glass.

Jesus in the World Today

We pray to you for healing for others, for the world
but in reality, we just want those problems to go away
we want the bad stuff and the bad news to go away,
we want the world to be perfect
just by praying.

Jesus, peace-granter,
we want to ignore racism and sexism and ageism and ableism,
we want to ignore how the earth is reacting to our gluttony,
believing the way we've always done things is still the right way,
even when day after day, we are bombarded with proof it's not,
even when we know your way is still not the way we do things.

Help us understand that healing takes time, takes commitment,
takes a change of heart and a willingness to change,
to do the work that you, Jesus, call us to do:
to welcome everyone, to live within our means
    and share our abundance,
to end inequality and unfairness,
to love one another as you love us.

Only through healing
our hearts and our spirits,
our attitudes and our mindsets,
our stereotypes and prejudices,
our insistence on being comfortable and familiar,
our persistence in ignoring the truth
dismissing facts and evidence
can we end suffering,
can we join you in the streets to bring compassion,
    peace, and mercy
to ourselves
to each other
and to everyone.

Amen

20. Grace Is Snacks and a Nap

ANNE LAMOTT WAS THE first person who writes about faith that I ever discovered. This happened in my mid-twenties, which means I've been reading her essays my entire adult life. Since she writes a lot about grace, she's likely influenced my thinking about it more than I realize. In her first collection of essays, in an essay entirely devoted to grace, she wrote, "It's the help you receive when you have no bright ideas left, when you are empty and desperate and have discovered that your best thinking and most charming charm have failed you."[97]

In my first book about faith and spirituality, I wrote that grace is to have "love and encouragement and the possibility of a fresh start already on offer when you show up. Grace is always there before you arrive, always waiting for you to take your seat."[98]

Grace is also elegance. Goodwill. A prayer before a meal. The name of my best friend's daughter.

Do you know what else grace is? It's an uncountable noun. There is such a thing. I discovered it after a conversation with my mother in which I said, so very profoundly, that grief is a person, place, or thing. Then I went off and wrote a poem with that title, and in the process of writing that poem I came across a teaching-related graphic that outlined eight different categories for nouns. Eight kinds of nouns! Proper or common, concrete or abstract, collective or possessive, countable or uncountable.

Uncountable nouns are things like sand, water, knowledge.
Wind, a.k.a. the Holy Spirit.
Grace.

Grace is particularly uncountable for the number of times it shows up in our lives, in the blessings and mercies, the miracles of our lives that we don't even recognize as grace.

You know why? Because Jesus never talked about grace, never used the word. For him, grace was a show-don't-tell kind of thing. He gave us the one big commandment: Love God, love your neighbors, love your enemies, and love yourself for cryin' out loud. But he never talked about grace.

He didn't need to because he *showed* us what grace is: the constant flow of love to everyone, with no judgment. Grace for all no matter who they are, no matter how messy and messed up they are, no matter how angry they make us, no matter how they hurt us. Remember how graciously he said, "Whoever has done nothing wrong can throw the first stone."[99] Because, as I might have mentioned before, love (and therefore, grace) is kindness and mercy, fairness and justice and peace, equality and equity, forgiveness and reconciliation, dignity and responsibility, acceptance and inclusion.

With boundaries, of course. Grace is also about setting boundaries.

Other than that, grace is about receiving what we need when we need it. Especially if it's not what we want. That's grace making us better humans. Better neighbors.

In a more recent book, Lamott wrote, "Sometimes the movement of grace looks like letting other people go first."[100] Like letting the person with a carton of eggs and a loaf of bread go before you and your twenty items at the grocery store checkout. Grace is in the small, forgettable moments as well as the big, significant moments. Like my favorites stories on social media about the professor who holds a student mom's baby for the entire lecture or the stranger who plays with a parent's toddler on an airplane (because it takes a village, right? And we're already kin.)

So, if love and grace are kind of the same thing—with grace having a teeny tiny bit of divine glow about it—why do we struggle with it? Specifically, why do we struggle to pay forward the grace we receive?

Grace Is Snacks and a Nap

Grace may be amazing, but we're not great at giving grace to others. We're not giving grace enough. We're not giving enough grace to others.

We expect grace for ourselves. We expect others to give grace to us, to cut us some slack, to be understanding and forgiving. And yet, we don't offer it to others. We resist. We withhold.

We are withholders of grace.

Like love, grace is about second chances, because we see the heart; second impressions because we see the hope; second guesses because maybe we misunderstood, missed the trying, missed the point of trial and error.

We don't consider the "learning opportunity" of mistakes and failures. We forget about the unforgiving power of first impressions. We don't offer second chances. One and done. Sorry, you blew it. We don't wonder about how someone slept, who said what as they walked out the door of their home, what pain is pounding in their head, what grief is grinding away at their guts.

We judge and assume, shame and reject in a hundred tiny ways.

At school, we teach the kids about kindness: Be kind, use kind words, have kind hands. At school, we tell kids it's okay to make mistakes: We all do! Try again! Keep trying! Your brain loves mistakes! Yet, beyond the classroom, outside the school, kids are often confronted with the opposite. They live in a world—at home, at hockey or cheer, in their neighborhood, at the babysitter's—that is not kind, does not use kind words, might not have kind hands, does not say or do kind things.

A world that does not offer grace to others.

Which is why the world needs more Jesus, even though he didn't speak the word grace. He didn't need to. Like I said, he *showed* it to us. Is that why he encouraged adults to be more childlike? He said (and I'm paraphrasing), "You need to be more like these kids. You need to be honest, you need to ask questions, you need to be in the moment and stop worrying about what you are going to do later. And also, have a snack and take a nap."[101]

Seriously, something to eat and a good night's sleep can really help you be a better human. Can really help you cut your neighbor some slack.

Jesus was not a withholder of love or grace, yet we are. We are stingy with grace and petty about mistakes because of our own insecurities. We are hard on others because we are hard on ourselves, because we are afraid there isn't enough grace for everyone, for us, especially, since we need it most. And yet, like love, grace can only be received by giving it.

Grace is appreciating what it took to do that—the thing, whatever the thing is you did or tried to do—in the first place, for the first time, from the heart, with the hope you get to do it again.

Author and artist Morgan Harper Nichols says so very simply, "Even here, grace abounds."[102] Even here, in the mistake, in the misstep, in the failing, in the falling, in the wishing it went differently, in the wondering what went wrong.

Grace is understanding and remembering that that happened to me, too, once. Grace is recognizing when courage and carrying on, carrying so much, are involved.

Grace is what you get when you think there is nothing left for you. You get what you need: an answer, a reason, a goal, encouragement, inspiration, support, reassurance, a person to talk to, a person who listens. A knot.

When you reach the end of your rope, grace ties a knot in it to help you hold on.

Here's something else about kids. They love to help. I mean, if someone (okay, me, who talks with her hands) knocks over the can containing the popsicle sticks that have everyone's name on them, at least four kids will rush over from wherever they are in the room to pick them up. Which usually ends up with someone getting hurt because they are totally focused on helping and not on keeping their noggins out of the way.

Jesus the teacher would say, "Help whenever you can, no matter where you are or what you're supposed to be doing *and* maintain situational awareness so that you don't make a new problem."

Grace Is Snacks and a Nap

Truly, though, I'm not being flippant about grace (or Jesus) because we need both so much. Actually, we have both, but we also have mud covering our eyes, and logs in our eyes, and our knickers in a knot (not tied by grace), so we tend to miss the moments when Jesus is in the scenario.

Kids love scenarios. In my work as a social-emotional learning teacher, we're always doing scenarios because they allow the kids to show how they feel about a situation ("A new friend invites you to a sleepover at their house") or to practice saying the right thing ("I'm sorry, it was an accident, are you okay?"). They know. They get it. Even if the word isn't in their vocabulary. The answer is always grace. Just like *we* know. We get what Jesus is saying. The answer is always grace. But the world, it's not so gracious. It's mean. It's digital. It's fake. It's artificial.

Grace is real. Because grace is a person, place, or thing. An uncountable noun. Like water and sand, knowledge and the wind. It's everywhere. In your body, in your bathing suit, in your hair, and in your mind. Look at that! We are all full of grace. We are giving off grace like sparks (also an uncountable noun).

Give grace, receive grace, have a snack, and take a nap. Keep it real. It's all that the Lord requires of you.

BLESSINGS FOR THE 21ST CENTURY

The crowd was restless
as Jesus walked slowly onto the stage

he wasn't sure what he was going to say
to this particular crowd
some of whom were his followers
and some of whom were simply
curious
because of what they'd heard about him

what do you say to people
when they need hope?
when they need a reason
to change their ways?
when they need to believe
it's possible to live in a new way
according to a new truth?

he stopped at the podium
and looked around at the people
sitting in the seats in front of him
their faces turned to him as they quieted
waiting
anticipating

what could he say that would
give them hope?

Blessings for the 21st Century

"You are blessed, you know,
you are blessed
even when you don't feel like it
you are blessed
and we are blessed by you

even when things are tough
and it seems like no one hears your prayers
we are blessed by your persistence

even when you are sad and alone
feeling lost and scared
we are blessed by your empathy

even when you are quiet
the last person to speak in a meeting
the last person to be picked for a team
just wait, good things will come to you
and we are blessed by your wisdom

if you are angry
because nothing seems fair
because nothing ever changes
and people with the power don't care
about the poor the sick the hungry
hang in there
it's happening
and we are blessed by your passion

when you offer food and clothing
visit people in hospital and in prison
sit with someone who is struggling
welcome people you've never met
maybe can't even understand
we are blessed by your kindness

Jesus in the World Today

when you shine your light into the world
when you come out to the world
as your authentic self
when you stand up for your friends and neighbors
instead of remaining silent
we are blessed by your whole-heartedness

when it seems like all anyone wants
is war
when landmines still exist
when land is taken from hardworking farmers
when people are shot simply for existing
just as their ancestors did generations ago
when bombs are dropped on hospitals and schools
and snipers line roads declared safe passages
when people born in other countries
disappear from the stores and the fields and the sidewalks
we are blessed by your attempts at making peace

if you are called weak for not working
if you are ignored because of your tears
if you are dismissed because you are shy
if you get arrested for protesting pipelines
if you are mocked for being kind for being real
for being spiritual for being joyful
if you are scorned for believing peace is possible
if you call out governments for weapons sales and war crimes
if you live in ways that make other people uncomfortable
if you speak in ways that make other people look away
if you want to make your own decisions for your body
we are blessed by you
by your existence
your courage
your perseverance
your love
your faithfulness

Blessings for the 21st Century

by your heart and soul and mind
by your strength."

Jesus stopped
he wasn't sure what else there was to say
he wasn't even sure what he had said

did anyone write that down?
is there a recording of what he just said?
will anyone remember?

will it make a difference?

Afterword: I Can See Clearly Now

IN 2002, MY FATHER was diagnosed with what we now call "early onset dementia." Dad was only 62 at the time of his diagnosis, and the progressive neurological disease took him quickly; he died at the age of 67.

I moved home to help my mother take care of Dad, and we kept him at home until his care became too challenging for us. I remember one evening listening from the kitchen to Mum helping Dad up the stairs. He struggled to lift each foot and put it down on the next step, and I could hear Mum saying, "Just put your foot down, just put it down." I went to look and saw my father taking these exaggerated steps, lifting his knee high yet seeming not to know how to put his foot down on the carpeted step. I had no idea what was going on, why he couldn't walk up the stairs, and it was becoming clear how difficult it was for him to continue living in their home.

Four years after his death, I spoke at a conference about being a caregiver for a parent with Alzheimer's. I also attended other presentations at the conference, including one by a doctor/researcher specializing in changes to vision and hearing in people with dementia.

When this person told us that someone with dementia loses depth perception as well the ability to differentiate edges and spaces, memories of my father flooded my brain. All of a sudden, so many of his behaviors and reactions made sense. If there had actually been a lightbulb go off above my head, it would have lit up the entire room.

That's why Dad couldn't see the stairs. Covered in dusty-rose-colored carpet, with his lack of depth perception and a narrowing field of vision, it wouldn't have seemed like there were stairs at all, perhaps just a steep slope. He would have been so confused—he knew what stairs were, but he couldn't see stairs, couldn't trust where to put down his foot.

When I heard all this at the conference, I became emotional at how we could have offered more compassion and appropriate care if we'd known better. What healing could we have brought to him, what suffering could we have avoided—for both my father and my mother—if we'd had more information?

My story about doing better when you know better reminds me of the story of Jesus healing the eyes of a man who was born blind.[103] That long and involved story is about both physical curing—the man could see after Jesus smeared a mixture of spit and mud on his eyes—and spiritual healing—how our perspective changes when Jesus opens our eyes to a new truth, a new way and a new life.

No matter what words we use to describe Jesus, ultimately, he was a healer. He wanted to heal our wounds as individuals, as communities, and as nations. To make each of us and all of humanity whole again, using love—compassion and mercy and fairness—as his medicine. To widen our vision, add depth and color and nuance in order to help us to see his dream for all humanity.

Clearly, I am arguing that the world needs more Jesus—but also that all we need is Jesus. Clearly, the more I write about this, the more I think about this, the more I see the way forward. I'm always curious why the words and ideas of Paul, who rebranded Jesus as The Christ, are considered more important (based on the frequency they are quoted and misrepresented) than the words and ideas of Jesus. Why do we need more than what Jesus said and did? We know enough about him, about his message and his mission, to follow him and transform our lives and the lives of others. All we need to know is what he told us to do: Love God, love your neighbor, love your enemy. Treat others the way you want to be treated.

Afterword: I Can See Clearly Now

Also, get some rest, eat some food, go for walks, and hang out with good friends.

It's all there, laid out for us in words and action. We already have the information we need to help and support and encourage and uplift others. Following Jesus should be easy, but we make it hard. We make it hard because we resist the truth, we refuse to see the better way. We make it hard because we know the right thing to do, but we just choose not to do it.

If we choose to judge, shame, reject and persecute others; if we lie and cheat and evade and manipulate for our own gain while causing pain to others; if we suppress and oppress and regress; if we remain silent and still and invisible, we are not following Jesus. There is no justification for anything other than love—compassion, mercy, peace and justice. There is no justification for ignoring Jesus' dream for humanity.

Jesus was not one to keep quiet when faced with the struggles and the suffering of others so look at who is posting, who is creating, who is talking, who is singing, who is calling out. Look at who is embodying love the way Jesus did. Fiercely, radically, bravely, and unapologetically. Be inspired, be encouraged, be motivated. Be transformed.

If you do all things with love, with courage, with enthusiasm for the chance to experience all the abundance of spirit that exists in us and around us and between us, then you are a manifestation of Jesus in the world today, in a world that needs Jesus and his law of love more than ever.

NOTES

Introduction
Butler Bass, *Freeing Jesus*, 266.

1. The World Needs More Jesus
2 A version of this essay appeared in the 2023 anthology, Following Jesus Today: stories and reflections, edited by Rob Fennell. https://rfennell8.wixsite.com/rcfennell
3 Mark 5:19, *TLB*

2. Knock Knock (You Know Who's There)
4 Hebrews 10:24–25, *NIV*
5 *Miriam-Webster's Collegiate Dictionary*, www.merriam-webster.com
6 Luke 11:5–8, *NIV*
7 Greenfield, "'Shameless Audacity,'" blog post.
8 Greenfield, "'Shameless Audacity,'" blog post.
9 *Miriam-Webster Dictionary*, online.
10 1 Corinthians 16:14, *NIV*
11 Matthew 10:34–39, *NIV*
12 Matthew 8:23–27, *NIV*
13 *Miriam-Webster*.
14 See https://introvertdear.com/what-is-an-introvert-definition/
15 Bell Hooks, *All About Love*, 92.
16 *Miriam-Webster*.
17 See https://www.britannica.com/science/radicle

3. Doing Jesusy Things
18 See https://science.howstuffworks.com/life/inside-the-mind/human-brain/baader-meinhof-phenomenon.htm
19 Bell, "Love What Matters Most," Facebook post, January 14, 2018. Used with permission.

20 Luke 10:37, *NIV*

4. We Hope It's Not Jesus
21 Hebrews 13:2, *NIV*
22 Peter J. Gomes, *The Scandalous Gospel of Jesus*, 197.
23 Matthew 25:40, *NIV*
24 Molly Phinney Baskette, *How To Begin When Your World Is Ending*, 113.
25 Luke 9:48, *NIV*
26 Matthew 5:3, *NIV*
27 Evans and Vaandering, *Little Book of Restorative Justice*, 8.
28 Chittister, *Wisdom Distilled*.

5. When Hope Becomes Subversive
29 Mark 11:17, *NIV*
30 See https://www.pbs.org/newshour/show/what-is-christian-nationalism-and-why-it-raises-concerns-about-threats-to-democracy
31 Kaitlin B. Curtice, *Native: Identity, Belonging, and Rediscovering God* (Brazos Press, 2020), 115, 117.
32 Marianne Williamson, *A Return to Love*, 190–191.

7. Jesus Is Political
33 Mark Sandlin, *Sojourners* 2013, see https://sojo.net/articles/10-things-you-cant-do-while-following-jesus.
34 Andy Stanley, "What Is Jesus' Take On Politics?" Youtube video. See https://www.youtube.com/watch?v=rGG4emresp4
35 John 17:22–23, *NIV*, author's italics.

8. Blessed Are the Fixers
36 Dyson, *Tears We Cannot Stop*.
37 https://earth.org/fast-fashions-detrimental-effect-on-the-environment/
38 Matthew 5:11, my paraphrase.
39 Buechner, *Wishful Thinking*.
40 Scott, *For All Who Hunger*, 150.

9. Turn the Other Cheek
41 Exodus 21:23–25 CEB
42 Adam Kirsch, *Is "An Eye for an Eye" Really and Eye for an Eye?* https://www.tabletmag.com/sections/belief/articles/daf-yomi-176

43 Matthew 5:38–40 *NIV*, my paraphrase
44 CBC Radio, *Ideas,* October 14, 2022. https://www.cbc.ca/player/play/audio/9.6443226
45 Munther Isaac, *Christ in the Rubble: Faith, the Bible, and the Genocide in Gaza,* excerpt at https://redletterchristians.org/2025/03/26/christ-in-the-rubble-an-excerpt/
46 CBC Radio, *Ideas,* October 14, 2022. https://www.cbc.ca/player/play/audio/9.6443226
47 Ibid.

10. Love the Earth
48 Matthew 25:35–36
49 Mercycorps.org, "How Climate Change Affects People Living in Poverty." See https://www.mercycorps.org/blog/climate-change-poverty
50 Luke 14:33, *NIV*
51 Mark 35:40, *NIV*

11. Plant What will Grow
52 Mark 3:1–6

12. Where Is Your Treasure?
53 J. L. Zagorsky, "Why Are People Hoarding Toilet Paper," *Social Science Space.* https://www.socialsciencespace.com/2020/03/why-are-people-hoarding-toilet-paper
54 Matthew 6:25–34, author's version.
55 Robin Wall Kimmerer, "The Serviceberry: An Economy of Abundance," in *Emergence Magazine.* https://emergencemagazine.org/story/the-serviceberry/
56 Matthew 6:21, *NIV*

13. It Doesn't Add Up
57 Matthew 11:28, *ESV* and *NIV*, respectively.
58 Matthew 26:11
59 Vakharia, *Math Therapy,* xix, xxiv.
60 Mighton, *All Things Being Equal,* pp.13-14.
61 Mighton, *All Things Being Equal,* pp. 43-44.
62 Mark 14:7, *CEB.*
63 https://www.vatican.va/content/francesco/en/messages/poveri/documents/20210613-messaggio-v-giornatamondiale-poveri-2021.html

64 https://united-church.ca/social-action/act-now/create-guaranteed-livable-income-program
65 https://basicincomecoalition.ca/en/what-is-basic-income/
66 https://www.cbsnews.com/colorado/news/denver-basic-income-project-first-year-report-significant-improvements-housing-outcomes/
67 Jasmin Arenas, "After 1 year, Denver Basic Income Project finds significant improvements in housing outcomes." https://www.denver7.com/news/local-news/supporters-of-denver-basic-income-project-call-for-more-funding
68 Neufeld, It Takes a Village," *Broadview*, March 2024.
69 Letters to the Editor, *Broadview*, June 2024.
70 David Fletcher, Instagram Threads, January 6, 2025. Used with permission.

14. Build a Bigger Table
71 Durrell Watkins, Twitter, April 14, 2019.
72 Barbara Butler Bass, Twitter, April 7, 2018.
73 Scott, *For All Who Hunger*, 219.
74 Curtice, *Native*, 83.

15. Audacious Women
75 Proverbs 31:10-31.
76 "Eshet Chayil (Woman of Valor)—Meaning, Translation & More." https://www.alephbeta.org/shabbat/eshet-proverbs-31-meaning-explained
77 Bessey, *Jesus Feminist*, 14.
78 Bessey, *Jesus Feminist*, 17.
79 Coren, *Rebel Christ*, 86.
80 Watterson, *Mary Magdalene*, 37.
81 Barr, *Biblical Womanhood*, 69–70.

17. Just Say Yes
82 Bono, *Surrender*, 48.
83 Acts 2:1–13.
84 John 20:19–23.
85 Luke 24:32.
86 Keefe, "Come, Holy Spirit, Come," *BeachTheology.com*, May 11, 2016.
87 Bono, *Surrender*, 521.

18. Part of Jesus' Family
88 Coren, *Rebel Christ*, 79.
89 Phillips, "The Bible Does Not Condemn Homosexuality," *medium.com* (blog), July 15, 2015.
90 Loorz, *Church of the Wild*, 145.

19. Healing Touch, Healing Tears
91 Mark 5:34, *NRSVU*.
92 John 5:1–9, *NIV*.
93 Interview with John Dominic Crossan, *Broadview* magazine, March 2020, pp. 16–18.
94 Bolz-Weber, "Do You Want to Be Made Well?" 2013.
95 Bessey, "Do You Want to Be Well?" *Field Notes*, March 28, 2023.
96 Mary Oliver, "Summer Day."

20. Grace Is Snacks and a Nap
97 Lamott, *Traveling Mercies*, 139.
98 Jewell, *Alphabet of Faith*, 75.
99 John 8:1–11, author's version.
100 Lamott, *Dusk, Night, Dawn*, 160.
101 Matthew 19:13–15.
102 Morgan Harper Nichols, Instagram post, February 2020.

Afterword
103 John 9:1–41.

Bibliography

Barr, Beth Allison. *The Making of Biblical Womanhood: How the Subjugation of Women Became Gospel Truth*. Brazos, 2021.
Bell, Jessica. Facebook post, January 14, 2018, https://www.facebook.com/jessica.bell.13/posts/pfbid0xX9bCvSAx4u4eegRbNSMN11v3jF8bm icybfcS8LZYKdsYhyNQ3DtRxFaWcZvoioDl
Bessey, Sarah. *Jesus Feminist: An Invitation to Revisit the Bible's View of Women*. Howard, 2013.
———. "Do You Want To Be Well?" *Field Notes* newsletter, Substack, March 28, 2023.
Bono, *Surrender: 40 Songs, One Story*. Doubleday Canada, 2022.
Bolz-Weber, Nadia. "Do You Want to Be Made Well? Man, I Wish Jesus Wouldn't Say Things Like That (A Sermon)." May 6, 2013. https://www.patheos.com/blogs/nadiabolzweber/2013/05/do-you-want-to-be-made-well-man-i-wish-jesus-wouldnt-say-things-like-that-a-sermon/
Broadview. www.broadview.org.
Buechner, Frederick. *Wishful Thinking: A Seeker's ABC*. HarperOne, 1993.
Bulter Bass, Diana. *Freeing Jesus: Rediscovering Jesus as Friend, Teacher, Savior, Lord, and Presence*. HarperOne, 2022.
CBC Radio, *Ideas*, October 14, 2022. https://www.cbc.ca/player/play/audio/9.6443226
Chittister, Joan. *Wisdom Distilled from the Daily: Living the Rule of St. Benedict Today*. HarperCollins, 1991.
Coren, Michael. *The Rebel Christ*. Dundurn, 2021.
Curtice, Kaitlin B. *Native: Identity, Belonging, and Rediscovering God*. Brazos, 2020.
Dyson, Michael Eric. *Tears We Cannot Stop: A Sermon to White America*. St. Martin's Griffin, 2017.
Evans, Katherine and Dorothy Vaandering. *Little Book of Restorative Justice in Education: Fostering Responsibility, Healing, and Hope in Schools*. 2nd ed. Good Books, 2022.
Fennell, Rob, ed. *Following Jesus Today: stories and reflections*. Robert C. Fennell, 2023.

BIBLIOGRAPHY

Gomes, Peter J. *The Scandalous Gospel of Jesus: What's So Good about the Good News*. HarperOne, 2024.

Greenfield, Craig. "'An Urgent Call for Shameless Audacity,'" Craig Greenfield blog, May 22, 2019. https://www.craiggreenfield.com/blog/shameless-audacity

Isaac, Munther. *Christ in the Rubble: Faith, the Bible, and the Genocide in Gaza*. Eerdmans, 2025.

Jewell, Sara. *Alphabet of Faith: 26 Words about Faith, Ethics, and Spirituality*. Wood Lake Books, 2021.

Kimmerer, Robin Wall. "The Serviceberry: An Economy of Abundance," in *Emergence Magazine*., October 26, 2022. https://emergencemagazine.org/story/the-serviceberry/.

Kirsch, Adam. "*Is 'An Eye for an Eye' Really and Eye for an Eye?*" Tablet magazine. August 30, 2016. https://www.tabletmag.com/sections/belief/articles/daf-yomi-176, 2016.

Keefe, Racheal. "Come, Holy Spirit, Come," *BeachTheology.com* (blog), May 11, 2016, https://beachtheology.com/?s=Come%2C+Holy+Spirit%2C+Come.

Lamott, Anne. *Traveling Mercies: Some Thoughts on Faith*. Anchor, 1999.

———. *Dusk, Night, Dawn: On Revival and Courage*. Random House, 2021.

Loorz, Victoria. *Church of the Wild: How Nature Invites Us into the Sacred*. Broadleaf, 2021.

Mercycorps.org, "How Climate Change Affects People Living in Poverty." April 10, 2018, updated April 8, 2021. https://www.mercycorps.org/blog/climate-change-poverty.

Mighton, John. *All Things Being Equal: Why Math Is the Key to a Better World*. Knopf, 2020.

Neufeld, Josiah. "It Takes A Village," in *Broadview* magazine, March 2024.

Oliver, Mary. "Summer Day." *House of Light*. Beacon, 1992.

Phillips, Adam Nicholas. "The Bible Does Not Condemn Homosexuality. Seriously, It Doesn't," *medium.com* (blog), July 15, 2015, https://medium.com/@adamnicholasphillips/the-bible-does-not-condemn-homosexuality-seriously-it-doesn-t-13ae949d6619.

Sandlin, Mark. "10 Things You Can't Do While Following Jesus." *Sojourners*. June 10, 2013. https://sojo.net/articles/10-things-you-cant-do-while-following-jesus.

Scott, Emily M. D. *For All Who Hunger: Searching for Communion in a Shattered World*. Convergent, 2020.

The United Church of Canada, "Create a Guaranteed Livable Income Program." https://united-church.ca/social-action/act-now/create-guaranteed-livable-income-program.

Vakharia, Vanessa. *Math Therapy: 5 Steps to Help Your Students Overcome Math Trauma and Build a Better Relationship with Math*. Corwin Press, 2024.

Watterson, Meggan. *Mary Magdalene Revealed: The First Apostle, Her Feminist Gospel & the Christianity We Haven't Tried Yet*. Hay House, 2021.

BIBLIOGRAPHY

Williamson, Marianne. *A Return to Love: Reflections on the Principles of a Course in Miracles.* HarperOne, 1996.

Zagorsky, J. L. "Why Are People Hoarding Toilet Paper," *Social Science Space,* March 19, 2020. https://www.socialsciencespace.com/2020/03/why-are-people-hoarding-toilet-paper